DEMENTIA UNTANGLED

A CAREGIVER'S GUIDE TO MANAGING ALZHEIMER'S AND COGNITIVE DECLINE IN LOVED ONES

LUNA CARTER

© **Copyright Luna Carter 2022 - All rights reserved.**

The content contained within this book may not be reproduced, duplicated or transmitted without direct written permission from the author or the publisher.

Under no circumstances will any blame or legal responsibility be held against the publisher, or author, for any damages, reparation, or monetary loss due to the information contained within this book, either directly or indirectly.

Legal Notice:

This book is copyright protected. It is only for personal use. You cannot amend, distribute, sell, use, quote or paraphrase any part, or the content within this book, without the consent of the author or publisher.

Disclaimer Notice:

Please note the information contained within this document is for educational and entertainment purposes only. All effort has been executed to present accurate, up to date, reliable, complete information. No warranties of any kind are declared or implied. Readers acknowledge that the author is not engaged in the rendering of legal, financial, medical or professional advice. The content within this book has been derived from various sources. Please consult a licensed professional before attempting any techniques outlined in this book.

By reading this document, the reader agrees that under no circumstances is the author responsible for any losses, direct or indirect, that are incurred as a result of the use of the information contained within this document, including, but not limited to, errors, omissions, or inaccuracies.

TABLE OF CONTENTS

A Free Gift To Our Readers — v
Introduction — vii

1. UNDERSTANDING DEMENTIA — 1
   - What Isn't Dementia? — 3
   - Types of Dementia — 5
   - Word of Advice — 10

2. BECOMING A CAREGIVER — 14
   - Educate Yourself — 18
   - Help Them Through the Initial Shock — 19

3. DAILY CARE — 25
   - Practical Tips for Task Management — 28

4. DEALING WITH CHALLENGING BEHAVIORS — 38
   - Walking About or Wandering — 41
   - Sexual Behavior — 44
   - Aggression — 47
   - Suspicion/Paranoia — 50
   - Refusal to Take Medication — 53

5. COMMUNICATION — 55
   - Communication Strategies — 57
   - Handling Curve Balls — 65
   - Communicating with the Medical Team — 68

6. HOME SAFETY — 70
   - Practical Tips — 71
   - Technology — 76

7. LEGAL, FINANCIAL, AND HOUSING MATTERS — 81
   - Health Care — 83
   - Financial Decisions — 85
   - Long-Term Care Facilities — 87

8. CAREGIVER WELLNESS	93
Coping With Emotions	97
Rewards of Caregiving	101
Conclusion	103
Leave a 1-Click Review	107
A Free Gift To Our Readers	109
References	111

A FREE GIFT TO OUR READERS

JUST FOR YOU!

18 ready-to-use templates that you can download, print, and start using right away! Scan the QR code or visit luna-carter.com

INTRODUCTION

Have you ever slept so hard that you woke up unsure whether it was day or night? The restlessness you felt then is what a person with dementia feels day in and day out. As hard as it is for them to deal with the situation, the caregivers also often feel burnt out, constantly under the impression of failing miserably at their job. Some days go by pleasantly, while others leave you completely drained. When the life of a loved one is at stake, it is natural to feel that way, though it is highly counterproductive, so to say. After all, you cannot treat a patient if you become one. So the first step while deciding to be a caregiver is to cut yourself some slack, to accept that you will make mistakes, that no one is perfect, and that it is okay to not be okay all the time. Dementia often hits suddenly, and its early symptoms get overlooked, especially among those living alone, due to stigma associated with it, limited resources, and lack of awareness in several parts of the world, which causes it to progress at a rapid rate. Among elders on other long-term medications, treatment of dementia gets even trickier. Currently, nearly 55 million people worldwide have Alzheimer's alone, 6.5 million being from America, with the numbers continuously rising as per the Alzheimer's Association. Hence, preventative measures and early detection go a long way.

Once detected, however, the road ahead gets more unstable since, unlike other diseases, patients with dementia require constant attention, patience, and understanding. If you are the primary carer of someone facing this issue, you are already doing a commendable job. If you are new to all this, consider this book a guide, a companion for herein, you will find a roadmap to tackle the possible challenges ahead, with practical tips to save you from being emotionally drained. After all, the first step toward helping others is to realize you need help too.

I know since this is how I felt when I started my journey eleven years ago as a caretaker of someone who meant the world to me—my mother, who was diagnosed with Alzheimer's. Born and brought up in Iowa, I had briefly left it to study in Chicago. My love for family brought me back. Years later, when my mother contracted the disease, I found myself alone. Having faced a lack of caregiver resources and guidance back in the day, I learned from my mistakes and trusted my gut feeling to lead the way. The first 2 years with my mother were relatively manageable since the symptoms were mild and far between. The next 6 years, however, kept me on my toes. During this time, my aunt too was diagnosed with the same disease. So my cousin and I joined hands to take care of both of them. After losing them both, I have continued to spread my knowledge and expertise on the subject to guide other caregivers by leading local support groups for caregivers, new caregiver workshops, and writing books for the past three years. My motive with this book is not to share facts alone but to help you through this difficult phase. When all else fails, it is the love we have for our family that sails us through. I shall begin by explaining what exactly dementia is before moving further to what you can do to help the patient and yourself in the process. I understand that the person for whom one decides to alter the course of their life is more than just a patient, but I shall use the word ahead for ease of understanding.

1

UNDERSTANDING DEMENTIA

The brain is a complex organ, which is compartmentalized into different lobes to ensure proper cognitive functioning, which includes motor skills, reasoning ability, emotional and sensory well-being, memory, and recognition. It also maintains the nervous system and hormonal balance and regulates other body functions. Dementia happens due to a malfunction in this system, that is, when the once-healthy neurons or nerve cells stop working, lose connection with other brain cells, and begin to die. Depending on the part of the brain that gets most affected, there is a personality change. This is the reason why two patients might not act alike. Some patients might face digestive disorders or trouble walking while others might have difficulty recognizing people, objects, or places or have hallucinations. The symptoms are mild and irregular in the initial stage and keep getting more evident as the disease progresses.

Though dementia is said to commonly occur at old age, according to the Population Research Bureau, Washington, as opposed to 2011, its affliction among people in America aged 70 years and above fell by 3% in 2019. In 2020, 7 million people in the country aged 65 or more had dementia. As per research over the years, women are said to be more susceptible to the disease than men. Education, loneliness, genetic mutations, and health conditions also affect mental health. A study suggests people with higher education levels are healthier. The possible reasons behind this can be higher cognitive skills and a better lifestyle such as a healthy diet and regular exercise. Dementia can also run in the family since genetic formulation and similar environmental conditions can be contributing factors. Lately, there also have been instances of COVID-19 affecting people with dementia more than healthy individuals. Even during the worldwide lockdown, constant fear and a sense of isolation contributed to worsened mental health.

Mr. A, an 85-year-old heart patient, was living a healthy life before COVID-19 hit everyone, forcing him to cease his routine morning walks. With a few of his friends consumed by the pandemic, his paranoia kept building up, and he began reading news reports obsessively while sitting alone in his house. Within a year, he lost weight, became weak, and later began showing signs of dementia. As per their family, it commenced with his belief that someone was not letting go of his leg. Though the family thought his leg had gotten stiff due to the cold, he later began insisting someone was there in his room. By the time a doctor was consulted, things had already started getting out of hand. They had missed the previous symptoms and dementia was already at an advanced stage. Some of his heart medication had to be kept on hold and he underwent minor surgery to remove excessive fluid from his brain. However, his older self kept withering away and within a year, he was gone.

While the pandemic led to a visible rise in heightened stress-related ailments, a need arose to make stronger bonds with each other to sail through difficult times. Depending on a person's age, general health, and treatment options, a person with dementia can extend their life span up to 20 years, if not more. Also, family support can make a huge difference. It is okay to seek information from others, but one must not lose hope reading or listening to others' stories. Stay informed, keep your tools handy, and have the strength to conquer one day at a time.

WHAT ISN'T DEMENTIA?

While self-diagnosis is the key to getting further help, it is imperative to not panic over minor instances of forgetfulness that we all experience in our daily lives. If you enter a room and forget what you came in for, it is probably because of your mind wandering somewhere else or being preoccupied. Your spouse might have told you specifically just now to get asparagus from the market but on entering the shop, it might have skipped your mind as you got busy talking to the shopkeeper. Similarly, forgetting the name of a stranger fifteen minutes after they told you is probably because the first time you weren't paying enough attention. Problems arise when you forget the name of your loved one or find yourself lost in a familiar space. While people, especially bilinguals, often forget less-utilized words or their spellings, a doctor needs to be consulted if they go entirely blank or recurrently forget commonly used names.

Also, several other diseases have similar symptoms and can get mixed up if not cautious. Delirium is one such ailment wherein the patient has delusions, hallucinations, disorientation, irritable behavior, and difficulty staying focused and recalling words. However, it is treatable once diagnosed. The main difference between delirium and dementia is the former worsens quickly and has more fluctuations within a day.

Fluid accumulation in the brain due to an accident, infection, or tumor can cause similar effects as that of dementia. Even hearing and visual impairments can lead to cognitive impairment. Another major cause can be a reduced supply of oxygen to the brain or proper blood flow in the body. Patients with lung, kidney, and heart diseases, as well as cancer also face episodes of unusual behavior. Undiagnosed liver cirrhosis patients are often recommended to visit the neurology department for showing dementia-like symptoms. Other issues include hormonal imbalance, diabetes, thyroid dysfunction, vitamin deficiency, and so on. Proper diagnosis and invasive tests must follow once any of the symptoms are noticed to rule out any other possibilities.

The diagnosis usually begins by getting general information about the patient and conducting physical, blood tests, and other related tests to monitor vitamins, minerals, and other essential bodily fluids. These follow further psychiatric and neurological assessments. The brain's common scans are Magnetic Resonance Imaging (MRI), Positron Emission Tomography (PET), and Computed Tomography (CT). Lumbar puncture is another method to analyze the fluids inside the brain. Though they might be costly and appear unnecessary at first, it is imperative to know for sure before looking at the treatment options. While a cure is not available yet, its effects and progression rate can be decreased with optimum medication and care.

TYPES OF DEMENTIA

Dementia itself is an umbrella term that encompasses four major kinds, though a person can have a combination of these as well. Once you identify the root cause, you can form a better understanding. So the next time your parent asks for the nth time where their car is, you won't get offended. They might not be distrusting you out of their free will, perhaps they don't remember having asked that question before. Here are the four basic types of dementia.

Alzheimer's Disease

Alzheimer's disease is the most prevalent form of dementia and occurs the most among people around 65 or later, though it can also manifest at a young age. Its root cause is the excessive production of tau and amyloid proteins. Tau proteins are responsible for stabilizing nerve cells in the brain but when they multiply beyond the optimum level, they form tangents inside neurons, disrupting communication and flow. Beta-amyloids make it worse by forming plaques between these nerve cells. In simpler words, it is more or less like a wall being formed in the brain due to excessive proteins hindering neuron traffic, thus causing chaos and ultimately neurons dying. When that happens, the patient's condition worsens. Even the size of the brain shrinks with time, causing further memory loss.

While an early onset can be a result of genetic mutation, among elders, this anomaly can be caused by several other factors such as diabetes, hypertension, head injury, Down's syndrome, and heart ailments. Moreover, a sedentary and isolated lifestyle, high blood pressure, cholesterol, obesity, hypertension, and a habit of smoking can also be plausible risk factors. Our genes play a part as well. The more relatives through generations one has who suffered from Alzheimer's, the higher the risk to others. However, in certain cases, the environment can also play a key factor in the prevalence of a particular disruptive gene. So a healthy lifestyle, which includes regular exercise, a nutritional diet, and social activities can reduce the risk of contracting the disease. Though the progression rate among individuals may vary, you can judge a person's condition based on the symptoms they exhibit. At an initial stage, they might forget about every single detail of a conversation you recently had with them. They might have no memory of bigger events also, such as a wedding they attended last week. They might ask you the same questions repeatedly, and have difficulty remembering common names. They might have trouble expressing themselves or dealing with numbers. They might also misplace things you find lying in an unusual place, for instance, a pen in the refrigerator. Their ability to take minor decisions would be affected.

However, as the disease progresses, these symptoms might get worse. They could wander off to places they no longer find familiar, they might have trouble sleeping and be irritable, moody, and suspicious to the point of being violent, or hallucinating. With time, these symptoms may come and go but you will see a considerable loss in their weight, memory, and bowel control and they would get entirely dependent on their caregivers for everything. Dysphagia is another outcome, in which the patient is unable to swallow food or liquids.

Though there is no permanent cure for this disease yet, doctors prescribe medicines to lessen the effects. The medication might vary as per the patient's medical history and symptoms. Antipsychotic medicines and antidepressants can also be prescribed in some cases. There are various therapies available too at various stages of Alzheimer's and other forms of dementia, such as Cognitive Stimulation Therapy (CST), sessions by occupational therapists or physiotherapists, memory cafes, and life story sessions as healthy exercises. Listening to music, painting, or indulging in other activities can also help.

Frontotemporal Dementia

As the name itself suggests, Frontotemporal dementia is caused by the shrinking of the frontal and temporal regions of the brain due to the accumulation of excessive tau and TDP43 proteins, causing a blockage and loss of brain cells. Most people suffering from this disease are in the age group of 40-65, though exceptions are likely. A genetic test is highly likely to be done in this case, though there are several cases with no family history whatsoever.

Most of the evident symptoms include behavioral and language issues. The former may be evident from a stark change in personality. A caring and an otherwise considerate person might suddenly appear coarse, aggressive, and heartless. They might even behave inappropriately such as stealing from others, using curse words, being sexually explicit, or having altered eating and personal hygiene habits. They might suddenly start showing a preference for sweets or at times even consume inedible items. As per the language issues, they might talk slowly, use incorrect word order or pitch, jumble up the sentence structures, and have trouble comprehending even their mother tongue anymore. You might even notice unusual repetitive behavior such as smacking their lips or clapping for no reason. People with this issue eventually become rather lonely and aloof. Like in the case of Alzheimer's, at later stages, they might be unable to use their motor skills efficiently or manage simple tasks alone because of weakness, body spasms, stiffness, lack of coordination, trouble swallowing, and controlling bowel movements. But handling them is a task as one has to ignore the insults and lack of empathy from the patient, which is clearly out of their hands. They might even put the caregivers through embarrassing situations, which must be handled with sensitivity.

But you do not have to bear everything alone since help is always around, be it in the form of house help, nursing homes, or social service organizations. Medications can vary according to symptoms. Antidepressants, antipsychotic medicines, and sedatives, along with occupational, speech, and language therapies, are some of the common treatment options. This disease too has no cure and proper care is needed for the patient to avoid further injury and infections.

Lewy Body Dementia

Also known as Dementia with Lewy bodies (DLB), this kind of dementia occurs due to the accumulation of excessive alpha-synuclein proteins (Lewy deposits) in the brain. These deposits kill neurotransmitters called dopamine and acetylcholine. Dopamine is necessary to regulate mood, and proper limb movement while ensuring optimum sleep, focus, and daily motivation. Meanwhile, acetylcholine manages learning ability and memory. When these messengers die, the body malfunctions. Lewy body dementia usually occurs among people beyond 65 years of age and is said to be more prevalent among men. It is one of the most common forms of dementia, especially in the United States. Parkinson's disease, rapid eye movement (REM) sleep disorder, and growing age can be possible risk factors.

One of its major symptoms includes hallucinations that are mostly visual rather than auditory. Violent tremors, body stiffness, constipation, and fainting episodes due to a sudden drop in blood pressure are also noticed. The patient may be constantly drowsy during the day and slow to respond but faces insomnia at night. Even during sleep, they might often act out, such as shouting or moving their hands and legs violently. They might even appear to be elsewhere in their thoughts as they sit in a corner, looking blankly in space. Memory loss is not a major factor until later, though they might feel confused more often with disorganized thought patterns and ideas. You might even notice altered body posture and multiple cases of falling. Depression can also be a part of this disease as patients begin to lose motivation in life.

Since some of its symptoms are similar to those of Alzheimer's disease, similar treatment options are used. One must consult the doctor to ensure proper medications based on symptoms and other long-term treatments since medicines for Lewy body dementia can react with them and cause severe side effects. Occupational therapies, speech-related and physical therapies can also prove useful. This disease is also fatal, and research is on to find better solutions.

Vascular Dementia

The root cause of vascular dementia is a lack of blood supply to the brain, which proves fatal to brain cells. It can be caused by blockage, damaged blood vessels, or a result of a major or several mini strokes. Diabetes, obesity, abnormal heart rhythm, high cholesterol level, smoking habits, unregulated alcohol intake, and age factors can also be possible reasons behind vascular dementia. This disease is more common in the United Kingdom and occurs usually after the age of 65. Heart patients, especially those who have survived an attack are prone to this ailment.

While its effects largely depend on the part of the brain

affected through the blockage, its common symptoms include slow thinking and decision-making process, trouble maintaining concentration, regular disorientation and poor posture, personality changes, and depression. They might be unable to control their bladder as well as their emotions. People with vascular dementia also often develop Alzheimer's disease or other forms of dementia, making the matter more serious. Memory loss may or may not be a key factor. Having another stroke may suddenly aggravate the symptoms, sometimes even causing partial paralysis.

Mini strokes are often not noticed by patients, but an MRI scan can put things in perspective. Since vascular dementia can go unnoticed, it is suggested that proper tests be conducted in case of stroke. The treatment of vascular dementia involves medication and therapies. The cells lost cannot be recovered but the degenerative process can be slowed down through timely treatment. The disease can meanwhile be prevented through regular exercise, healthy eating habits, maintaining optimum blood pressure and cholesterol levels, reducing alcohol intake, and quitting the habit of smoking.

WORD OF ADVICE

You might have noticed that dementia, currently, is termed as a progressive, non-curable disease and the life span of its various types may vary from 2 to 20 years on paper but you need not take it as a final word. The symptoms can worsen quickly or at a slow pace. Your loved one might have more willpower than you had anticipated. They might have mild symptoms for the most part, or not. Keep a close tab on the changes in their behavior and look out for any negative effects of the prescribed medication. Whenever in doubt, seek professional help. Share as many details as you can with the doctor for their better understanding of further treatment.

It might seem scary now, but adversities often make us realize the inner strength we didn't know existed. Take the first step and you will continue to find your way. You might feel alone sometimes but your loved one is there still, noticing you trying with all your might to help them through. Even if their older self seems to be long lost, on the inside they are struggling ceaselessly. Their pain will always supersede yours. Use this as motivation though, not as an excuse to neglect your health and needs. I will come back to this part in Chapter 8.

The first thing to keep in mind before deciding to be someone's caregiver is ensuring everyone in the house is on the same page and if you can spare enough time to be there for the patient to avoid future arguments, especially when bringing someone home. It is a big decision that is going to affect all. Having honest conversations while dealing with everyday situations can help. Instead of dwelling on the problems, it is better to discuss possible solutions while keeping in mind their long-term effect. Say you cannot take their rude behavior anymore, will you be okay with letting them move to a health center or would you regret it later when your anger subsides? There is nothing wrong with the decision, especially once the patient's condition worsens since they would be in professional hands; though many people believe it would break their heart, forcing them to live in an unknown place, away from their loved ones during their final moments. But for others, it is unbearable to see them this way and they think they are not able to do enough. The decision is entirely yours.

Also, do not expect everyone to take the news sportingly.

You might find yourself alone most of the time, but this is how the world is. Appreciate help and understanding but don't expect it from anyone. Relatives are usually the first to disappear in times of need. Some of your friends might wish to help but don't know where to begin or how to approach you without sounding offensive. Even if it's a text message from someone, a simple call to know your well-being, or a visit bearing something homemade, appreciate it since such people are not easy to come by. Many caregivers do not like to impose and prefer handling things themselves. But you must not wait for things to become worse before you seek assistance. State your needs clearly and accept if someone volunteers to look after the patient while you run an errand. If it makes you feel better, you can return the favor later. That's what relationships are all about.

Every day isn't alike and hence, it is understandable for every person to get frustrated once in a while. You might need a break to organize your thoughts and there is nothing in it to feel guilty about. Experts call it a necessity and not a luxury to take care of your own mental and physical health. This way, you can increase your work efficiency and be better at your job. Friends, family, voluntary workers, or adult daycare facilities can take over during some parts of the day to help you spare some time for yourself. You can even hire a house helper for added assistance. Have a forgiving attitude toward the patient as well as toward yourself. No caregiver is perfect. We all make mistakes. Learn from your mistakes and move on. Analyze what agitates them and avoid using it again. Therapeutic lying can be an essential tool to reduce stress. For instance, if someone they know has recently passed away and they can't remember having attended their funeral, it is better to keep it that way. The lies are not aimed at benefiting you directly but the patient, hence it is in no way a selfish act. You have to accept that some lies are better than harsh truths, especially when dealing with a patient. Keep your sentences as simple and direct as possible. Rationality, logic, and reason have to be subsided at times. Always remember that you are dealing with the disease and not your loved one, so trying to explain the logic can end up worsening the situation. It is essential to understand that the patient is not pretending. This is the main reason why diagnosis usually gets delayed. If you notice regular unusual behavior in anyone you've known for years, do consult a doctor. Ask yourself if your loved one would have said what they said in a normal circumstance.

If you have children in the house, be open and transparent with them about everything. Depending on their age and temperament, they might react differently to the changing circumstances in the house. Keep them on board and tell them to not take anything personally. One's parent suffering from dementia might seem perfectly fine one moment but then suddenly say something hurtful to their child. Encourage your children to be expressive and share their experiences with you so that a solution can be found. Remind them that their grandparent is unwell, but they love them, nevertheless. If elders are not honest with the kids, they might feel anxious, afraid, angry, blame themselves, or feel unloved in the long run. With better understanding, however, they can also prove useful by keeping the patient busy, say by playing board games or listening to music with them. This will make the children more responsible and empathetic toward others and the patient would not feel lonely and lost. I will discuss some of these topics in detail later, but let us begin by discussing first things first.

2

BECOMING A CAREGIVER

It is one thing to know about a disease but to imagine it altering the life of your loved one is unbearable. It takes time to accept the new reality and come to terms with it. If someone close to you has been diagnosed with dementia, take your time to process the information. Discuss it with the patient and give them space. In rare cases where the patient's condition has already deteriorated, do not share sensitive information with them before consulting the doctor. If you've recently noticed a few symptoms and fear them being a sign of dementia, do not jump to conclusions before all the test results are in. Let the doctor do their work. Our first reaction to hearing bad news is usually disbelief. We want to get a second opinion, be really sure. There is nothing wrong with it. Get further tests done or share reports, and be doubly sure before moving further. As discussed before, it might not necessarily be dementia after all.

If it is, though, anger, frustration, and regret might follow in any order, and you might blame yourself for not doing enough. The patient is most likely regretting themselves for not being cautious or as active as they should have been. However, for some, the news comes as a relief since they finally get the answers they had been looking for. Living in the dark is worse than knowing the exact cause of one's predicament. Most often than not, relief, regret, and frustration hit together and further aggravate the situation, causing a panic attack, anxiety, or symptoms of depression in the patient or those attached to them. It is essential to understand that several factors are responsible for dementia to occur and there might be nothing they could have done differently to avoid it. Even if they could, it is impossible to go back and make amends. Life is transient and we are mere mortals who have to accept reality eventually. We cannot stay in denial or grieve over it endlessly for the only way is forward. No matter how hard it might seem at first, facing your fears and accepting your emotions will make you stronger and give you clarity of mind. Even the most intense emotions will pass, and you will be ready to take the next step, though it might take some time. Everyone processes traumatic news differently, but here are some tips for guidance if you find yourself entirely lost.

- **Cry it out.** Keeping your emotions bottled up can cause more pain and trouble. If the emotions are not dealt with properly, they keep resurfacing and eventually consume the person. Crying is not a sign of weakness but strength. Acknowledge your emotions, even if it is in front of your loved one, as this honesty will make your bond stronger and can help you understand them better.

- **Do not neglect your health.** Take a deep breath and divert your attention toward the process of breathing in through your mouth and breathing out through your belly. This will regulate your heartbeat and blood pressure. Do not forget to hydrate yourself. Some people handle stress by working out or going for a long walk.

- **Prioritize yourself.** Sleeping over it can also clear your mind since overthinking can be mentally exhausting. Cancel unimportant meetings or take an off from work, if possible. Let the dishes pile up. Don't pick up that unnecessary call. You do not have to handle everything at once.

- **Contact your support group.** If you have a close friend or relative to confide in, it is good to take their advice or simply vent out what is in your mind. Hearing them out can also put things in perspective. However, choose wisely since the wrong person can make you feel worse. Ensure the other person cares about you and has the mental space to deal with your problems.

- **Seek professional help.** You can even talk to the doctor, a counselor, a religious person in your community, or someone who has previously dealt with a similar situation. Do not talk to random strangers or open unverified internet websites or pages that can potentially contain misleading information.

- **Write it down.** Get yourself a journal or a simple diary and jot down whatever you feel. Let your emotions flow as eventually, it will make you feel better. You can even write it all on a piece of paper and burn it down later if you wish to keep it private.

- **Distract your mind.** You can get into activities that usually prove cathartic, for instance, indulging in a hobby such as painting or crocheting, or simply driving yourself to a certain place that helps you organize your thoughts.

- **Be mature and responsible.** Do not harm yourself or do something you would regret later about. Drinking profusely or consuming something else can give you momentary peace but that is not the solution to your predicament. Reflecting on the situation rather than running away from it can help one heal faster.

- **Pray for your loved one if you are a religious person.** In times of dire situations, several people find solace in the belief that a higher power is there to rely on. Don't ask for a miracle though, just accept the reality, do what you can, and leave the rest to God.

Remember that your loved one is still there, and you still have time to make it right. We all feel wronged and often curse our destiny for having made us suffer this but then again, it isn't only us. If you look around, you will always find yourself in a better condition than many people in the outer world. Hope sustains the universe. Don't lose it or you shall lose yourself. Recall your memories with this person and think about all that you can still do for them. Once you have reached acceptance, you can move ahead.

EDUCATE YOURSELF

If the news has affected you to the core and you wish to do something about it instead of crying over the spilled milk, take the next step: Read up everything you can on the disease. If your loved one has Lewy body dementia, for instance, get more knowledge about the condition and how it progresses. This can help you prepare for future challenges, reduce stress, and you would be able to foster reasonable expectations. As discussed before, proper and timely medication, lifestyle changes, and therapy sessions can slow down the progress of dementia considerably and improve the patient's quality of life. Meanwhile, if the condition is reversible, then effective measures must be taken to alleviate it. The best ways to gain information are by reading books, watching videos and documentaries, accessing fact sheets released by various organizations, attending online training sessions, and joining workshops. Detailed resource material on every type of dementia is widely available today for use. Find a local or national dementia association or get yourself a helpline number for assistance. You could even talk to other caregivers and learn from their experiences. Interacting with them can help you decide the next course of action better and avoid the mistakes they might have made initially. People dealing with similar issues are often more reciprocating and helpful, giving them a perfect opportunity to learn from each other.

However, since the symptoms of two patients may vary, the treatment plan must be tailor-made and subjective. As the primary carer, you are responsible for collecting and imparting information, and determining roles everyone in your circle is likely to play. Having first-hand interaction with their doctor, keeping a record of their treatment plan and symptoms, and being aware of their history and traumas, you will have a better understanding of the next course of action than anyone with half knowledge. Talk to friends and family members who might know them better. Ask them about their past and share current details, encouraging them to be mindful and consistent with their behavior toward the patient. Your emotional stability would play a key role in effective management since there would be people depending on you for help and guidance. Hope for the best, but think through the worst scenarios to avoid being overwhelmed during a time of need. Be realistic but do not let it show to the patient for they are prone to depression, considering they already know about their health condition. Your job is to ensure they are happy, occupied, and distracted enough to stay clear of dark thoughts as much as possible. If you have trouble controlling your emotions, seek assistance for your own good. It might be the most horrible phase of your life, but it is also a great learning experience for you, which you will realize more years later.

HELP THEM THROUGH THE INITIAL SHOCK

Once you get a hold of your emotions and have gained enough knowledge, make a rational plan to handle the immediate crisis without getting ahead of yourself. You do not have to plan everything at once, but you need to bring changes to make their life easy. There is no surety how the patient might react to your approaching them, but you have to make them understand your point. It is comparatively easy to make plans with the spouse or someone else already living with you but convincing someone to leave their house can be a task in itself. They might not want to let go of their house or neighborhood, they might not wish to be treated as a burden, and they might feel they can handle the situation themselves. Honest conversation is the key to success here since living alone might not be a viable option for them anymore. It is generally perceived that a social setup can help any patient cope with the situation better and they can receive practical assistance too. From visiting a doctor for regular checkups, getting groceries, and ensuring the tap was turned off to changing their clothes, everything is likely to become impossible to manage alone in the near future. But you cannot force their hand, at least not right away. Leaving one's house can be a big compromise since people have a sense of belonging in their own space and their sense of comfort lies in the rooms, furniture, and even in their own neighborhood. For a person with dementia, it can be extra hard to move into a house they don't feel connected to. So let them make their own decision, though you can help them reach out to you instead of bottling everything up and assure them their decisions will be honored and respected.

Try to be as patient as you can with your loved one with dementia as they are also processing the information. Most patients feel stigmatized and dislike being treated differently. You do not want them to feel that way about you or they shall isolate themselves further. They are still the same as they have always been. The disease doesn't define their identity or alter it, for that matter. Even if they seem to waver, remind them of their achievements and how you still need them as you did before. In any case, choose your words wisely as sometimes, even when our intentions are good, things can go sideways. In an emotionally charged situation like this, it is likely to happen as well, so organize your thoughts before approaching them. Do not tell them everything will be fine or that they must stay happy or look at the bright side but assure them you are there for them in whichever way they require and give them practical tips that can help. Nudge them to open up to you about their desires and fears. You can even reach out to the friend they confide in to know what their fears are to find viable solutions.

You might have done your homework and know more than the patient about their condition, but it is better to let them speak. Keep a diary to jot down details and wishes they might have, probably in their own handwriting so that you both can refer to them later. A journal can also be maintained to keep accurate track of their symptomatic advancements for better assessment by the doctor. If they are in an early stage of dementia, discuss legal, financial, and healthcare matters with them as these can be a major cause of their stress currently or later on. See Chapter 7 for an in-depth discussion on making plans.

Another way of helping them through the difficult scenario is by creating a thorough plan and implementing it. Some of the ideas are listed below.

- Ensure information about the doctor is easily accessible to them in case of an emergency.
- Engage them in planning dietary changes.
- Sign them up in social groups to find the ones they can relate to.
- Arrange family outdoor trips since nature is a great healer.
- Make them follow a proper routine.
- Ensure they are properly hydrated, something that can easily skip their mind.

Patients with a fatal disease often develop an inclination toward *carpe diem* and wish to leave a legacy behind to be remembered as the wholesome person they were before the disease consumed them. So based on their interest, they can join age-appropriate classes, such as pottery, dancing, meditation, and the like, or create something for their future generations, such as a memoir, recipe book, or draw a family portrait. These activities can keep them occupied and happy, and exercise their cognitive skills effectively. The task must be chosen to ensure their physical and emotional well-being rather than just passing time. Above all, doctors often insist that the patient must have a proper routine that they follow religiously, such as a fixed time of morning walk, breakfast, social sessions, lunch, and so on.

As the disease progresses, your loved one would most likely be dependent on the primary carer for maximum tasks but at the initial stage, they would most likely prefer having the command in their hands. Dignity and individuality mean a lot to every person, after all. Be supportive but do not overindulge. Let them pay their own bills or manage their daily chores. If you feel they are forgetting to attend a meeting or a session, inform them like it just came up instead of making them feel embarrassed. It is imperative to keep an open mind and change your behavior, including the percentage of indulgence, as the disease progresses. For instance, the patient might like it initially but later begin to get agitated when asked what they wish to have for lunch. If you notice a change, stop asking that question anymore. Regular meditation or other relaxing activities can build emotional strength in a caregiver to stay calm during challenging situations.

When deciding their daily routine, keep in mind their social and cultural background, their religious and spiritual preferences, and their desires. If they are spiritual, you could look up classes nearby. Honor their sense of risk-taking, confidence, self-esteem, and sense of accomplishment while ensuring safety standards are maintained to avoid injury.

Also, some activities may be effective yet exhausting for them. Their interest and efficiency are likely to fluctuate as well, hence keep your plans fluid while ensuring consistency in the routine itself. Their attention span would also vary with time, so exercise the skill of having their undivided attention when you say something to them. They might not agree with everything you say, hence keep an open mind and have patience instead of forcing anything upon them. Don't argue. Accept reasonable demands and deal with the rest discreetly. They might want to go out alone but if they are likely to forget their way back, have someone accompany them or go yourself. Understanding both the verbal and non-verbal needs of the patient is imperative. The world around can be a nasty place, especially for a vulnerable person. Hence, keep an eye out for emotional or mental trauma, misbehavior, or neglect by others and be their shield wherever possible.

Caregiving can prove beneficial for not only the patient but also for their family members. For the patient, it can be a chance to spend time in the company of people they know, and they won't feel as displaced as in the case of a health center. A happy attitude can add to a patient's life and increase their life expectancy. They can learn a skill they never got time for before by joining classes or trying it at home with the help of the internet, such as baking. Physical and emotional comfort, inclusion, and a sense of security can make them feel better. Moreover, being socially active can help them open up and it can add to their confidence, besides giving them a sense of purpose. Taking a life-altering decision to be a caregiver can also be fulfilling in the sense that it represents one's love for the other person. There is no other reason why a person would put themselves through such an inconsistent task. It is a learning experience that can change one's life for the better, and give them a purpose and a sense of fulfillment. I have seen people in life who lost their loved ones in an accident, some of them don't even know for sure what happened to them. Living with that regret for the entire life of not being able to do anything or say goodbye can eat up a person. In the case of dementia, however, you still have time to make a difference and spend quality time with them. In the long run, it even makes you appreciate your own life more and have compassion. Since children learn more from watching their parents rather than being preached to, it can set a good example for them to grow into kind and considerate human beings.

It does not have to stop with the passing of a loved one either. Several individuals keep helping others by imparting knowledge and expertise they have gained throughout the years. It gives them a new purpose in life, builds a sense of community, and makes the world a better place. Even if later on you decide not to stay active with the cause, you still come out of it a better person.

3

DAILY CARE

The early phase of dementia is mostly manageable. However, as the disease progresses, your role as a caregiver is likely to become more hectic and challenging since the cognitive and behavioral functioning of your loved one would begin to decline, along with motor skills in some cases. This would lead to the inability to carry out basic life functions without assistance, commonly known as activities of daily living (ADLs), such as bathing, dressing up, grooming, managing oral hygiene, toileting, eating, walking, and so on. Apart from these, instrumental activities of daily living (IADLs) also decline at this stage. Such activities involve more complex tasks such as driving or using public transport, preparing food, managing finances, shopping, taking medicines, doing laundry, and answering the phone. All these skills are negatively affected by the decline in:

- **Memory:** They might partially or entirely forget about activities they regularly did before, such as managing their phone, ironing clothes, or bathing. They might forget important dates and recent events. Wandering in the house is another symptom, which makes it harder to venture out alone. They might also misplace things often.

- **Executive functioning:** They might mix up the sequence of a task at hand and have trouble organizing items and thoughts, for instance, messing up their signature recipe or bathing ritual. Multitasking becomes exceptionally difficult. This deteriorates at earlier stages and is more linked with IADLs.

- **Judgment skills:** They might have trouble deciding which clothes to wear on a particular occasion, such as a sunny day or a winter evening. You might notice them wearing a winter cap at 40 degrees outside or mismatched socks. Taking mundane decisions might appear like a Herculean task.

- **Visual-spatial skills:** They might have trouble judging distance or identifying objects and colors, their function, and placement. This can prove harmful while driving as there can be higher chances of an accident. They might even forget what a toilet seat is meant for. They might not see it at all if the floor, walls, and toilet seat are all the same in color.

- **Knowledge of time and place:** They might confuse day with night or summers with winters and repeatedly forget where they are. They might mix the years or believe they are younger. They can easily get lost in a familiar building or forget where they parked their car. This is most likely to happen at an advanced stage of dementia.

- **Attention span:** They might tie half the buttons of their shirt and then get immersed in something else. They might also forget to turn off appliances, thus inadvertently threatening their own lives, along with those of others. Concentrating on a conversation for long might also be a task.

- **Behavioral and psychological well-being:** They might get agitated, suspicious, or fearful of anyone trying to assist them with their daily chores. Their mood swings might be unpredictable, and they might be prone to apathy and depression. This is a direct effect of their inability to manage simple tasks.

At intermediate and advanced stages, independent living can become increasingly difficult. The patient would require constant vigilance and attention. What makes it more complicated is that they are aware of their deteriorating condition, and it can further impact their mental health, causing severe anxiety and embarrassment, thus creating a vicious circle that is hard to break. Several studies, however, suggest that the ability to perform IADLs declines first among people than ADLs. The primary carer, hence, has to closely monitor these changes so that a doctor can understand the extent of functional decline in the patient. Another way of determining it is through cognitive tests. In the case of Lewy body dementia, motor skills such as the ability to walk properly are also affected along with cognitive and behavioral alterations. Since the inability to walk properly is assumed to be a physical issue rather than a neurological one, proper assessment can become difficult. As per a study conducted in Taiwan, it was seen that at an initial stage, patients required more assistance in transportation than the rest. It was argued that the reason could be more autonomy to venture out initially than at later stages due to deteriorating health.

PRACTICAL TIPS FOR TASK MANAGEMENT

To help the distressed patient, a caregiver needs to tackle situations wisely. By understanding the condition of your loved one, you can judge whether they can single-handedly finish a task or need assistance; and if they do, to what extent. Doctors usually advise not to let the patient drive a vehicle early on in the case of dementia. Hence, your loved one might seek company to reach their home or other places. It is advised to get their consent early on to transfer their authority, to someone they trust, to take vital decisions. If they have put their faith in you, handle it responsibly but remember that you cannot excel in everything. In some situations, if you feel they are not comfortable with you or if you can't handle something well, you can seek help from a regular practitioner, dentist, physiotherapist, occupational therapist, dietician, family, or friends. A patient's routine and habits may vary according to their likes, hobbies, past job history, and experiences. A gym trainer might insist on continuing to handle heavy weights; while an interior designer might wish to move furniture in the house. Refusing them straight away, getting angry, or trying to reason with them can worsen things and make them agitated and distressed. The best solution is to improvise. Based on the dementia type and stage, the symptoms and requirements of patients may vary. Your involvement in their daily routine is likely to keep increasing with time. so be flexible in your approach and find new methods to deal with common situations. Here are some of the points to keep in mind while creating a daily schedule for your loved one.

Schedule Wisely

Fixed schedules for daily chores ensure maximum output and the more active they are during the day, the better they would sleep at night. Avoid daytime napping as much as possible. You can also have a fixed toilet routine for them based on their diet and early habits. Their diet must have maximum liquids during the day and minimum at night. If they are physically fit, include outdoor activities such as walking, yoga, Tai Chi, or a game they like playing. If they are good with words and need to keep their mind sharp, interest them in a game of Scrabble. You can get them their old tools in a box and interest them in sorting them according to size or color. Schedule tasks requiring more energy early in the morning when the patient is fresh, and use the evening for mild activities that do not require too much attention. Excessive alcohol and caffeine intake can cause health issues and insomnia or disrupted sleep patterns. Do not let them have coffee at night.

Promote outdoor activities for socializing if they feel comfortable with it. You can visit a sports stadium, theater, mall, party, or family function with them. As discussed before, one can explore memory cafes nearby to meet fellow people with dementia informally and have pleasant discussions with them. You can even invite their close friends and family members home for company and to relive memories. Based on a person's cultural and ethnic background, there is a difference in community-building activities and events. Attending them can make them relaxed. As the disease reaches its final stage, they might prefer to stay home, so the schedule must change according to their symptoms and preferences. But during the initial and intermediate stages, more interaction with others can keep depression and anxiety at bay.

Some part of the day must be devoted to looking at old family photos to rummage through the past. Music can also bring back old memories. Take cues from their career to understand their interests better. Puzzles, board games, physical strength training, and gardening can be as fulfilling for them as mundane household jobs like folding clothes, reorganizing kitchen cabinets, or washing a car. Every little achievement can produce a happiness hormone, called dopamine. Spending time with kids and pets can also add happiness and a sense of comfort to their life.

However, the task must not appear too childish to them. At an early stage, they can easily handle the stove and knives, so telling them to peel off oranges as you do the rest can hurt their sentiments.

Understand Their Needs

Be mindful of their requirements and fears while designing their routine. Check their bathing preferences and try to use them, such as a tub or faucet. Fix the water temperature to avoid accidental burns. In terms of clothing, you might not like their usual dressing sense but if it gives them satisfaction and a sense of confidence, honor it. At an advanced stage, you can substitute their usual clothes with those that are easy to take off by them, you, or the attendant. Ensure that they are in safe hands to avoid mental trauma and abuse. Install a low-powered bulb or light source in the room at night or keep a flashlight by their bedside to avoid tripping while going to the bathroom at night.

If your loved one constantly scratches their skin, they might have increased sensitivity and dryness issues. Ease their predicament instead of trying to stop them. It can be due to extra hot water or a block of harsh, fragrant soap. Reduce their bathing time and install a humidifier in their room. Use cold compresses and mild ointment over the affected area. Trim their nails regularly so that they do not harm themselves.

The chair they regularly sit on while resting, working, or eating must be at the proper height and sturdy to ensure proper eye level and prevent falling, and joint pain. Bean bags, recliners, and rocking chairs can be uncomfortable or scary for them. If there is a continued issue with their balance, get them a wheelchair to move around.

The patient might forget to eat and drink at all or might overdo it, so keep a check on their dietary pattern and the possible causes behind the abnormality. Some medicines can affect the appetite of a person. If they have forgotten that they ate just an hour ago and ask for lunch, give them something light and healthy to eat. Keep healthy eatables such as nuts and fruits all around the house to promote snacking so that they do not get starved. You can also give over-the-counter vitamins and other supplements after consulting the doctor. Check the temperature of everything they consume beforehand since it can burn their mouth or cause brain freeze. Keep items that might be mistaken for food, including detergents and other chemicals, out of reach. Throw away stale food and expired medicines regularly. Use unbreakable utensils to avoid accidents.

Promote Healthy Habits

At the initial level, if they are fussy eaters, give them their favorite foods after consulting their dietician. Encourage them to eat fruits and vegetables with high nutritional value. Use less salt and sugar in their diet, especially for patients with diabetes or high cholesterol levels. Even if they don't like an ingredient, which is otherwise necessary for them, use it discreetly in the recipe. Give them a high-fiber diet for proper bowel movements and plenty of fluids for optimum hydration, such as different juices, squashes, smoothies, soups, and shakes. Green leafy vegetables contain important nutrients that are good for brain health. Some studies also suggest including Mediterranean food, beans, berries, nuts, cereals, and whole grains in the diet. While seafood and chicken are good, avoid saturated fat, commonly found in red meat and dairy products such as cheese and butter. Use olive oil for cooking. A diet plan must be as per their activities.

Sit together during meals to make eating a fun and engaging activity. Play with colors in terms of food, and crockery to make the food look appetizing and appealing. If they have trouble chewing the food, give them semi-solids or feed them in small chewable bites. Even slice the fruits into small pieces. If they cannot swallow properly, consult a speech-language pathologist.

Taking them to the park regularly for a walk and meditation as physical activity can make them feel hungry. Sitting in a park and doing gentle breathing exercises can promote good health. Regularly monitor their general health and body language to know if a medicine does not suit them or if any food item reacts with the former. If they take responsibility for their medication, help them organize their pills for better understanding. Write the day and time on the boxes to avoid confusion. Keep following up as eventually, it would be your job entirely. When they begin getting confused or forgetful about it, keep the medicine out of their reach to avoid overdose.

Ensure Cleanliness

Based on the weather and personal habits, decide if they need a daily bath and manage accordingly. If they cannot bathe alone or if you notice bruises after a bath or something amiss such as shampoo not properly washed off from their scalp, be with them to guide them while ensuring a safe distance to maintain their dignity. At an advanced stage, keep them comfortable and in control of the situation by regularly asking if they are doing okay while bathing them yourself. A towel bath can also be used to keep the patient clean. Consult your doctor to get guidance on it so that the patient doesn't get threatened. If they are uncomfortable with you or if you cannot bring yourself to do it, seek professional help.

If they mix clean clothes with the used ones or forget to do laundry, take it upon yourself to wash and dry their clothes regularly. If they refuse to change their clothes, insisting that they like the dress a lot, you can purchase a similar pair for them and use it alternatively.

For personal grooming, you can take them to their regular shop or do it yourself with safe tools, as per requirement. Remind them to brush their teeth regularly to avoid gum and digestive issues. For elders, it is essential to keep dentures in a good condition. Visit a dentist regularly, if possible. If there is a recurring issue with continence, use adult pads or briefs. You can also guide them to the washroom if you feel they cannot find it.

Watch out for spills on the floor to avoid tripping. Keep their glasses half full and give them food in small quantities to avoid wastage and spilling. Cover up the table with cloth, paper towels, or a plastic sheet that can be cleaned easily after use. Take care that they are skid-proof.

HANDLE DISTRACTIONS

Keep their room and closet clutter-free to avoid confusion. You could regularly update it as per the season and take away bulky cardigans and coats if your loved one appears frailer than before. If you feel they are scared of mirrors or cannot recognize their image anymore, cover them up. This happens when their short-term memory gets affected and they believe they are younger than the person in the mirror.

This can cause confusion and distress. Sometimes windows with glare also have to be covered up to prevent glare.

A tablecloth and mat with intricate patterns can confuse them, so use solid colors. Do not ask them what they wish to eat or give them too many food options at once. Bring starters and main course one by one. To hone their decision-making skills, however, you can ask them to choose one item from the two and see their reaction. At an advanced stage, even simple cutlery can become difficult to use, so keep a minimum of utensils at the table. If they have trouble using a spoon, either show them how to use it or give them food they can eat without a spoon, such as a sandwich. Watching television or playing loud music while eating can create confusion. Hence, having meals in a quiet room is a good option.

Keep unnecessary furniture out of the way to avoid falls and bruises as their vision, muscle strength, and balance might suffer. When it comes to difficult situations, such as your loved one trying to go out at odd hours, distract them with another discussion to divert their attention. Do not tell them they can't go out as it would confuse them further. If they tell you they wish to go home, ask them what it looks like rather than telling them they can't go back.

Provide Guidance

Encourage autonomy by giving them simple tasks. Direct them to take the first step and move on to the next one after the first step finishes. You can use verbal language and pictures, or do it along with them, such as brushing your teeth at the same time. Use simple and brief sentence structures, and give them positive feedback after every step. If their executive functioning is affected, guide them with the appropriate sequence during tasks. Do not confuse them with unnecessary decision-making, such as choosing what to wear or eat. Give them fewer options for less confusion.

Use post-its and other cues all around the house to guide them when you are not around so that they do not feel lost. To wander around in a safe space such as the house can help them stay mobile and interact with others. Let them move around. We shall discuss it further in the next chapter. While traveling alone in public transport in the initial stages, give them pictures of home or street in case they forget, address details, and emergency contact details. Tracking their phone can also be a good option to stay in the loop. Initially, words are enough but as the disease progresses, more detailed guidance and uninterrupted vigilance would be required.

Keep Pace With Them

If they have a short attention span, ensure eye contact while talking to them and remove any possible distractions in the room. They might be slow to process the information they just heard or read and even slower to implement it. Be patient and encouraging at every step. Don't cut them off while speaking lest they shall forget what they were saying. If you are in a hurry, let someone else be with them rather than expecting them to be quick.

While cooking something, give them a task they can finish at their own pace without safety hazards. Understand that the result might be unusable, non-flattering, and late but make them feel they have been helpful and brilliant. Their taste buds are likely to change from time to time, so they might not like their once-favorite dish anymore, for instance, people who earlier liked spicy food more might prefer sweets now. Find their current inclination and use it wisely. If they insist on eating something specific, give it to them but in the appropriate quantity as per the doctor. Encourage slow eating to ensure food gets chewed well before swallowing.

Some patients have bad dreams regularly at night or suffer from insomnia. If they wake you up late at night, ask them what the matter is instead of losing your cool. If they have digestive issues, give them the prescribed medicines. Continued insomnia can be treated with sedatives under the doctor's guidance. Having prior knowledge of handling emergencies can be helpful. Keep the doors properly locked at night to avoid them wandering off. Keep objects with sharp edges, such as forks, knives, and showpieces out of their reach. Pistols, if any, must be always kept in a safe.

ENCOURAGE PARTICIPATION

Active participation in activity can keep the patient invested and happy, though nothing substantial comes out of it. Follow proper safety measures. Let them chop vegetables if they remember how to use a knife. If they don't, give them something simple, for instance, whipping egg whites with a spoon. Even if it spills, they won't get hurt. Let them work at their own pace. As long as they can do a task themselves, no matter the speed, let them continue instead of doing it for them. If you feel they are tired, take a break and continue later. Cutlery with long handles is often easy to use.

If they are religious, take them to the church or other spiritual places regularly. If they cannot take the exertion anymore, make arrangements at home, such as playing spiritual music online for them. Social activities involve both formal and informal meetings and sessions, the former including paid memory classes, discussion groups, cognition classes, and the like while informal get-togethers can be organized with friends and family.

Repeat it to yourself time and again that you are dealing with a patient and not your spouse, father, grandmother, or anyone else that used to be a few years ago. The person in front of you might appear normal sometimes but for everything out of the ordinary they do, there has to be an explanation behind it, and more often than not, it is dementia in this case. Note down the new developments and even if your method of tackling them the first time was bad, learn from them and tell yourself how you can improve the next time. We're not born with magical skills to cook, drive, paint, or even sing. We learn these skills as we grow old. No parent is perfect with their kids. It is all a learning process. Learn every day and be better at your job instead of losing hope or blaming yourself for mistakes you make along the way.

4

DEALING WITH CHALLENGING BEHAVIORS

If you break down every possible symptom of dementia, you will find that the solutions also vary. This is because the brain is a complex organ managing the entire nervous system and is responsible for vital body functions. It is like the central processing unit (CPU) of a computer. One can treat minor bodily malfunctions effectively with medicines, diet management, and lifestyle changes. But when the mind causes trouble, it gets difficult since no medicine can give instant relief and the symptoms come and go frequently. There is an added prejudice and misinformation about brain-related diseases, mostly because of the unpredictability of the patient's reaction sometimes. As difficult as it is to deal with some situations during dementia, there is usually not enough appreciation at the end of it. Even if we tell ourselves we are dealing with a patient, the harsh words said sometimes get too much to take. Your loved one's sense of reality is entirely different from yours. You might not be able to change behavioral issues, but trying to understand where they are coming from and which strategies you can implement to tackle them can improve the situation. Be objective and before taking any action, ask yourself if the behavior is simply embarrassing, disruptive, and uncomfortable or whether it poses a direct or immediate threat to their own lives or those of others. A sudden change in behavior or mood is most likely due to a trigger. Either they need something or are stressed and unable to express it. While some individuals may feel relaxed meeting people in crowded areas, others might get frightened or restless. COVID-19 also created a fear among some people to mingle with others. As we established earlier, social interaction is beneficial for them. But if it constantly proves counterproductive, there is no point pushing it further.

At times, there is some physical issue but they do not know how to put it in words, and hence behave weirdly. If the cause is successfully identified, a solution can be sought easily. If they cannot tell the cause themselves, you have to find the possible cues and reach a conclusion. At times, the condition is similar to that of a newborn, the difference being their cue to cry it out instead of showing peculiar behavior that is hard to identify. As dementia progresses and such symptoms begin to increase, you have to be vigilant all the time. Note down every single detail, everything out of the ordinary that you notice throughout the day. Ask yourself what has changed that could have possibly triggered behavior. If they are too quiet and distant, it might be because their best friend, who earlier visited every day, hasn't been around lately. If they constantly refuse to drink anything, it might be because they are losing control of their bladder and find it embarrassing to pee in their clothes. The grandmother of a friend I know would eat very little and refuse beverages since she could no longer handle her weight and feared falling on the way to the bathroom.

In some cases, a changed behavior might be an indicator of an underlying problem, which if goes unnoticed, can be a health hazard. When words begin to fail them, your loved one might be unable to express their pain through sentences. Perhaps they do not know what is happening to them. Observe their movements and facial expressions. If they wince while standing up or walk slowly, see if there is an injury in their leg. Touch the possible trigger location gently and see if they react. If their breathing is faster than before even while sitting, get their blood pressure checked immediately. If they have a history of another long-term disease, such as asthma or diabetes, make it known to the attendant, if you hire one in your absence, so that they have an idea about the possible causes, symptoms, and precautionary measures. If the pain persists, consult a doctor and tell them the clues you have collected to conclude. It would help the doctor to make an effective prognosis before conducting further tests. If the patient has diarrhea, it could be due to infection or a reaction to some medicine. To be sure, ask yourself if their medicine was recently changed or if there is something different they ate, which didn't suit them. If they have no problem swallowing or digesting but still refuse to eat certain foods, there could be an ulcer in their mouth. A thorough investigation is always a must in such cases since incorrect diagnosis and medicine can do more harm than good.

Another major issue, commonly seen in people with Alzheimer's in the intermediate or later stages is sundowning syndrome, in which the patient begins getting restless as the sun begins to set. They might get aggressive, paranoid, suspicious, or wander around, screaming. Sundowning syndrome occurs with lack of sleep, less to no exposure to sunlight, and health issues, among other reasons. We will discuss all these behavioral and psychological symptoms of dementia (BPSD), and methods to handle them effectively. Always remember that in the later stages, the truth might hurt them mentally and emotionally or not register in their mind at all. Distraction and lies are going to be your essential tools to cope.

WALKING ABOUT OR WANDERING

While walking about has a purpose, wandering is often without one. People with dementia often walk around in the house. You might not see any reason behind their constant movement but for them, there is always a purpose. Also, initially, you might find it a harmless exercise to stay active, but it can become a challenging situation if not monitored. During day time, since doors are open and there is traffic outside, they can be hard to find if lost. At night, since everyone is asleep, it is hard to keep a tab on their activities. Someone I knew had a habit of making tea for themselves at night. After they had dementia, they would still often insist on making tea and would often forget to turn off the burner. As a solution then, an induction stove was installed and a bell next to the kitchen door rang whenever someone entered it. We might not always understand the reason behind their moving about, so here are some of the possible ones to ponder upon.

- They wanted to go to the kitchen but forgot where they were going midway because they got distracted.
- They have to pee but cannot find the washroom.
- They are looking for their shoes but cannot find them anywhere.
- They wish to talk to someone in the house but cannot find them.
- They are looking for someone who is no more.

- They wish to go back to their old home or cannot find their car.
- They have woken up in the middle of the night and think it is morning and wish to go for a walk.
- They do not remember having left the job and wish to go to work.
- They saw a pizza box and since they used to deliver it in the past, they think they are supposed to deliver it.
- They saw the door and wished to explore it.
- They are bored and want to socialize with others.
- They came across the car keys and instinctively rushed outside.
- Their leg hurts and they think moving it can make it better.
- They feel they can leave the pain behind if they move about.
- They are feeling restless or agitated (read "Aggression" below).

Trying to walk out of the house for some reason is called exit seeking. Walking about or seeking to go out is not an unhealthy habit if kept in check to avoid accidents. It ensures mobility and physical exercise and gives the patient a chance to mingle with others and have a sense of independence and belonging. However, if they have a history of falling, balance issues, hearing, or a visual impairment, walking unsupervised can become an issue.

Always ensure their shoes properly fit them and are easy to wear. Do not let them walk on uneven surfaces. Keep their belongings, especially the ones they regularly use, in plain sight. Keep a digital clock by their bedside that tells them the date and whether it is day or night. Keep the doors locked at night and try, if you can, to keep the main door out of sight by giving them a room far away from it. You can even hide the main door using curtains, pictures, or sign boards to stop. Some people even suggest keeping a black doormat in front of the door that resembles a giant hole they might fall into. Keep the car keys hidden. Give them an identity card in case they get lost in the street somehow. Keep your neighbors informed about their condition so that they can report back if they notice them wandering around. GPS bracelets are also available to track their whereabouts if they have a habit of wandering. For details on technological safety measures, read Chapter 6.

Ask them if anything hurts and consult a doctor. Identify the cause of their restlessness; it might be due to unfavorable noise, temperature, or light. If they ask for their relative who is dead or have a wish to go back to their home, do not tell them they cannot reach them as this would cause them pain. When their short-term memory suffers, they sometimes time-shift, that is, they imagine themselves living in the past. Such behavior is particularly common among people with Alzheimer's at later stages. It's preferable for you to keep some of their furniture and other belongings in your house, especially in their bedroom so that they can connect with them. Call them by their name often so that they remember who they are. If they miss their house, show them those items. Ask them what their home looks like or show them pictures of their old place or the concerned relative so that they can relive past memories and feel content.

To ensure a good night's sleep, do not let them take a nap during the day. Do not give them caffeine, especially past evening. Keep their dinner light and devoid of excessive fluids so that they do not wake up for a bathroom break. Keep them engaged in meaningful activities throughout the day so that their energy is efficiently utilized, and they have a sense of purpose. Take them out in the sunshine for a change of space and fresh air. Regular exposure to sunlight can also decline the chances of sundowning. Take calculated risks. In the first stage, if you feel they can manage alone, let them go to the park if there is no traffic on the way. If there is, drop them at the gate and give them written instructions to stay there till you come back along with your contact details. Later on, ensure someone is with them always, beside them, or at a reachable distance to give them some independence, if they seek it.

SEXUAL BEHAVIOR

Human beings require a safe space and relationships to grow and feel loved, and wanted. Sexuality is one such form of expression and forms an intrinsic part of our needs. A person with dementia might also seek that closeness but fail to express it with words or channel their urges. Hence, they might use direct or implied methods that are socially unacceptable to express themselves. Some patients become entirely disinterested in sexual activities to the point of apathy while others feel more inclined toward them and need an outlet for their sexual and physical tension. They might sit close to someone, touch or stroke their hand, or give them a gentle kiss on their face, arms, or hands. Based on cultural and religious contexts, this behavior might be frowned upon. A complete lack of inhibitions, however, is a result of further cognitive impairment, change in personality, and lack of judgment and leads to behavior such as the use of obscene language, sexual advances toward a partner or someone else, touching themselves, masturbating, or disrobing. There can also be a sudden change in the sexual orientation of the patient. Inhibition loss is most common in patients with frontotemporal dementia. As per some studies, among men, such behavior is mostly physical while among women, it is mostly verbal in form. The possible causes behind such behavior, however, are not always a need for sexual intimacy. It can also be due to:

- discomfort in their genital areas
- tight clothes
- overcrowded or restrictive atmosphere
- high temperature in the room
- an expression of loneliness
- misidentifying the person they misbehaved with

If not handled well, the situation can get worse. For instance, excessive and uninhibited masturbation can massively hurt their genital area. Confrontation can lead to aggression while taking no action can cause them harm or put others in a difficult situation. This can be embarrassing and distressing for the carer and other family members. At this juncture, some people decide they can no longer handle the situation and opt for professional help. Societal judgment forces others to confine them in closed spaces. However, some couples continue to have a healthy physical relationship for quite a while in some cases, diversion and other common solutions prove helpful.

If the patient is your spouse with dementia, consult your doctor if they have any physical pain or other health condition. Also, proper safety measures, such as cleanliness and the use of condoms, are essential to prevent infections, which can be common in the case of dementia. Even during the act, the patient might appear distant, cold, or insensitive. Sometimes, the patient likes intimacy but their libido becomes non-existent, which can be frustrating for the partner. Talking to someone you trust and seeking help can make you feel better. See Chapter 8 for more discussion on the topic. Consent must always be the unsaid rule for both partners before getting ahead with anything. When the patient's ability to make decisions gets affected, it is better to handle the matter more carefully. Sexual arousal is not a testimony of consent unless other non-verbal signs clearly state what they wish. Be sure of the laws in your country on consent before pressing the matter further. Remember, consent goes both ways. If you are not comfortable with your partner's advances anymore, seek help from the practitioner, family members, or police in the worst scenario. Their demand for sex can be rather a need for intimacy and if rejected straightaway, can be a cause of aggression or distress.

In the case of a parent, this situation can be more complicated. Several medical treatment options and multi-disciplinary actions are available, but their efficacy varies and there is a risk of side effects, especially among elders. Hence, it is advisable to take an informed decision.

If you continue to deal with the situation yourself or with the help of an attendant, investigate the cause before moving further. Check for physical afflictions such as infection or simply the need to use a washroom. Check the themes of their daily entertainment sources and make amends, if necessary. Create a diversion from the immediate situation with another activity or take them to another room. If their advances were toward an attendant, try hiring another one of the opposite genders. Next, educate yourself and your family members to deal with the situation effectively. Keep their hands occupied with recreational activities. Give them a soft toy or a stress ball. Keep a pillow in their lap as a barrier. Divert their attention toward activities involving physical touches, such as a foot, head, or back massage. Brush their hair. Avoid leaving young kids alone with the patient. Give them clothes with buttons or a zipper at the back to prevent them from touching their genitals. Let their clothes have pockets. Stuff these pockets with objects they can touch.

If your parent meets someone new during a social event or at a dementia care facility, ensure that it is consensual and safe. Understand their need for intimacy and be supportive of their decisions. Make sure safety standards are followed and efficiently maintained. It is imperative to have an open mind and an unprejudiced approach to the matter and understand the needs of your loved one. However, be extra cautious of them being taken advantage of since they are vulnerable to abuse.

AGGRESSION

Anger and aggressive behavior among patients often rise over time. It can cause unnecessary tension in the house and can have a lasting effect on the psyche of the caretaker. With a patient, an abrupt change in mood might be a result of some recent event or an unmet need they are unable to express in words. There might be a problem with their immediate surroundings, such as:

- excessive darkness in their room
- trouble moving around the house
- room temperature too low or too high
- excessive noise in or around the house
- overcrowding in the room
- feeling of loneliness
- clothes too tight or too loose
- uncomfortable shoes

Another cause can be a recurring confusion about their deteriorating health, control, and independence. They might get agitated whenever they forget someone's name or cannot recall a word. If they have always loved being independent, the sense of constant dependency can be frustrating for them, and they might insist on breaking free. Some people might get restless when left alone while others might seek company. The sudden rise in aggression can also be a possible side-effect of a change in medication. Apart from this, health issues that can trigger anger include:

- unbearable pain
- digestive issues, such as constipation or diarrhea
- rise in temperature
- stomach or urinary tract infection
- inflammation
- insomnia
- hallucinations or delusions

No matter how polite your loved one was throughout their life, they can become someone entirely new when mad. Aggression can be verbal in the form of foul language but if you engage, it can quickly turn physical. They might shout or threaten you or throw abuses you have never heard from their mouth before. They can even break household items, and use physical violence such as slapping, pulling hair, hurling things, or biting. However, understand that the rules we follow while dealing with individuals in our usual life do not apply here. You must be careful while approaching the situation and act responsibly to avoid the situation from getting out of hand. As an initial step, try to identify the cause behind their behavior. As you enter their room, check the surroundings for discomfort. Notice their movements and touch them gently, maybe while offering to massage them, to check if anything is hurting them. Do not ask too many questions at once or press them for answers if they don't have any as it would make the matter worse. Do not try to reason with them by telling them everything will be okay. If they feel misunderstood, they might get more frustrated. If they are slightly upset, sit in front of them, probably in a similar manner as they are sitting, and talk politely while maintaining eye contact. This will make them feel calm. Talking loudly or standing cross-armed can mean you are trying to fight.

Redirect them from the cause of contention. Take them for a ride, a walk, or just out of their room for some time; so that they forget about what is troubling them and rather focus on something constructive. Play light music, sing along, and dance with them if they are up for it. If you think they are too tired, help them get some sleep. Everything will be fine once they are well-rested. Involve them in a task and tell them you need their help. If you feel they cannot operate their smartphone anymore and get agitated whenever a notification comes or someone calls, take it from them and say you will fix it for them. Instead of talking further on the same matter, divert their attention toward something they might like, such as watering the plants. Keep the phone out of their reach and tell their friends to call you instead. You are not being cruel here but caring as irritation and anger are negative emotions and their persistence can negatively affect their mental health. When the thing of contention, the smartphone here, is taken out of the picture and their mind is diverted to the gardening process, they would feel relaxed.

If the situation gets worse, take a step back. Even if they begin shouting or screaming, do not raise your voice. Do not confront them or try to reason with them; instead, leave the room for a while and come back when they calm down. Tell yourself it is not about you and that they are mad at something else. Tell yourself it is not your fault and try to understand their situation. Consult a family member, healthcare worker, or general practitioner on the further course of action. Doctors sometimes add antipsychotic medicines temporarily to handle excessive aggression but look out for their possible side effects. If you find yourself in an extreme situation that could threaten your life or that of your loved one, you can even call 911 for immediate action. Do inform them that you are dealing with a dementia patient.

After it all has passed, be your normal self with them. If you can't forget everything right away, discuss your emotions with someone you trust or a psychologist but do not talk about it with the patient. They might remember parts of it or not at all, but it is best to leave that memory behind them as it was not their fault. Read Chapter 8 to know further about managing your mental health in difficult situations.

SUSPICION/PARANOIA

Delusions are common among people with dementia, which refer to a perceived notion not based on truth. If they feel threatened by these delusions, paranoia can quickly take hold. Their imagination can be wild and based on past experiences or earlier fears magnified out of proportion. These can also be due to a tale twisted enough by their mind to become something else. Delusions are the most common among people with Lewy body disease and the least in frontotemporal dementia. Major delusions include:

- being watched
- being lied to
- being conspired against
- being robbed
- hate mongering against them
- someone trying to harm them
- partner having an extramarital affair

- impersonation

They might feel someone has stolen from them or is trying to steal. It is most likely because your loved one kept their belongings in odd places and cannot remember them. Even a customer care text can cause alarm as if someone is harassing them. A patient with Lewy body disease would get paranoid at balance messages from his bank, saying they knew how much money he had in his account and that they were trying to steal it from him. Another common delusion arising from the inability to recognize known spaces or people is the belief that they are being kept captive by imposters. It can also be due to time-shifting. They might insist someone is spying on them. They might refuse to eat due to the fear of being poisoned.

These suspicions can have a massive effect on their mental stability and cause a rapid decline in their cognitive ability. They can even be aggressive against the supposed culprit. Simply telling them they are wrong can make them believe you are also involved in the conspiracy. The acquisitions can be constant and demeaning but one must not take them personally. Some parents accuse their children of being imposters after their short-term memory gets impaired. They might remember the house and their children from when they were young and not recognize you. Even if most of what they say proves untrue, verify the facts anyway to know the exact cause behind it. Another possible cause behind such behavior is trouble with their senses (hearing, listening, or seeing), poor lighting, or a reaction to some medicine.

An effective solution can be listening to them carefully and acknowledging their thoughts. You could also agree with them and politely suggest another possibility while assuring them you will investigate it further to be sure. Appear serious and sincere even if you are lying to their face because the situation is real and upsetting for them. If they fear the food is poisoned, involve them in the preparation or make them see it being cooked. The more they are involved in social activities and stay busy, the less suspicious they will become. If their paranoia has built on something they saw on the television, turn it off.

If they cannot find something, help them locate it. If they regularly lose things, take it upon yourself to organize their belongings. Keep them at a spot where they are easy to locate. However, do not change too much in the house. Keep the house clutter free and add post-its wherever needed. If they seem to have lost money, quietly put some at a random place and then tell them you have found it. Make extra copies of important items such as keys or documents that are often mislaid. If they commonly lose their favorite shoes, purchase an extra pair.

If your loved one constantly looks into drawers and cabinets, looking for something, or hoarding items, lock the ones you think contain potentially harmful substances, such as chemicals or kitchen knives. Create rummage bags or boxes to redirect their attention toward happy memories. Keep it at a place where they go most often. You can also use the drawer they usually check. You can fill it with an old cell phone, letters, photographs, greeting cards, or something related to your loved one's old job that brings back happy memories. It can have old trophies, achievement certificate copies, an address book, or a treasured gift. A rummage box can also have their favorite pair of trousers, the first wallet their spouse gifted them, or the Uno you used to play with when young. A distraction kit, on the contrary, can have items that can intrigue their senses, such as a tape with pleasant music, a comic book, a coin purse, a comb, a perfume, or a scented candle. Always remember that what works today might not be good enough tomorrow. Hence, keep updating these boxes and kits regularly.

REFUSAL TO TAKE MEDICATION

Dementia is a progressive disease, which means it gets worse with the passing of time. Medications, though necessary to slow the process, cannot cure the disease entirely. What's worse, they have occasional side effects and have to be changed from time to time. A person having any ailment is liable to get frustrated and tired of taking medicine if it does not make them feel better. With dementia, however, this frustration is just one reason behind the refusal to take medicine. Other possible reasons include:

- trouble swallowing
- nausea or other side effects
- unpleasant smell or taste
- horrible after-taste
- suspicious about medications
- can't understand what to do with the medicine
- confusion if there is too much commotion in the room

Ensure there is silence in the room and no distractions while giving them medicine. Make it a part of their fixed routine and tell them what it is for. You can even take your own vitamins at the same time to put them at ease. Be patient with them and let them take it themselves. If they do not remember what to do, guide them or make them mimic your actions. If they are anxious about taking multiple pills together, give them one by one and keep the capsules and bottles out of their sight. You can even give it a rest and come back after a few minutes to try again. If there is a particular time when they are the most irritable, talk to the doctor about it as some medicines can be given at alternate times during the day.

If the patient refuses to take the medicine at all, it is best to consult the doctor. There can be a valid reason behind the patient's reluctance, such as a side effect causing them discomfort. In elders, side effects are common and mild doses are recommended. Also, there is a chance of their long-term medication reacting with that of dementia. Common side effects include nausea, vomiting, dizziness, fatigue, indigestion, muscle cramps, or insomnia. The doctor can be in a better position to judge if they know the exact cause of refusal. If the size of the medicine is the issue, it can be replaced with a liquid tonic or patches. Some medicines can be crushed as well before use but consult the doctor before taking this decision. You could even give them something to eat after the medicine to balance out the bad taste, such as fennel seeds or a piece of chocolate. Some doctors suggest giving the medicine discreetly, camouflaged in their food. This decision, however, must not be taken without medical approval.

5

COMMUNICATION

Communication is a means of expressing our emotions and feelings with others to build strong and healthy relationships. Effective communication involves both verbal and non-verbal methods and is a complex process of listening, interpreting, and forming an appropriate response. Language forms a part of our core memory since we grow up using it in oral or written forms and influences our mood and perception of life. The left hemisphere of the brain is responsible for language (Broca's area) and speech comprehension (Wernicke's area). Both areas are connected to each other through neural pathways. Word recognition and speech are also managed by other parts of the brain. However, in dementia, with the rapid loss of neurons, these areas begin getting affected. For instance, with damage to Broca's area, known as aphasia, the brain loses its ability to understand complex sentence structures. The effect on these parts of the brain can be detected through imaging techniques. At times, the person with dementia faces other issues that either distract them or cause trouble responding, such as shooting pain, delirium, depression, or affected sense organs. By understanding the exact cause behind language impairment, an effective plan can be made for effective treatment. Dementia damages the following functions:

- **Communication and cognition**—A patient might have problems in acquiring and interpreting knowledge as per their experience and observations. They might also fail at conveying their thoughts effectively through words and gestures.

- **Memory and focus**—They might not remember recent events or people. They might end their sentence midway, forgetting their trail of thoughts; or keep repeating themselves. They might also have trouble staying focused on a conversation.

- **Language skills**—They lack lexical resources and hence, frame short and incomplete sentences. They might have difficulty organizing their words into meaningful sentences or forget common words, especially in the second acquired language. As a substitute, they might use fillers (that thing), and offensive words, or create new words to convey the meaning. They might also not remember using slang, idioms, or proverbs.

- **Visual perception**—Dementia often has an effect on semantics, such as the power of recognizing words and visualizing them. Also, toward later stages, the ability to read and write suffers. They might see something but still not recognize or register it. They might not recognize what right or left means or identify colors anymore.

- **Problem-solving skills**—They might be unable to analyze complex information and come up with a possible solution, such as how to untangle their hair after a wash. Even making simple choices can become impossible since their functional memory gets affected.

People with vascular dementia have affected motor skills, language, and speech disturbances. As the patient is aware of their shortcomings, this negatively affects their sense of pride and independence. To avoid making embarrassing mistakes, many people speak less or not at all during the later stages of dementia. With regular assurance, encouragement, and a respectful attitude toward their feelings and emotions, this issue can be resolved. Never mock them for forgetting something. Get them regularly checked for hearing, or visual problems and get them hearing aids and spectacles, if needed.

COMMUNICATION STRATEGIES

Though communication skills begin degenerating early in dementia, symptoms may vary from person to person. Some strategies must be used at all times as a method of practice while others can be inculcated as the disease progresses. As short-term memory gets affected, they might even begin to lose their command over any other language they might have acquired over the years and prefer conversing in their mother tongue. This can be fine with family members fluent in the language but for others, there can be difficulty understanding them. The patient can also be either too loud or nearly inaudible while speaking. This can even be a result of hearing issues or trouble speaking, which some patients develop at later stages. For a caregiver, it is essential to understand the importance of effective strategies to convey their message effectively. If the patient has begun forgetting common words, you can create simple exercises to refresh their memory. However, if the semantic knowledge source is considerably damaged, simple strategies would not work anymore. Take the help of non-verbal, paraverbal, along with sensory cues to get through to them. Some strategies for effective communication are discussed below.

Limit Distractions

As discussed in the last chapter, distractions can cause trouble in concentrating. If there is too much noise around while you are trying to convey something, your loved one is likely to get distracted and not understand you properly. In some cases, they might even mix up the situation, for instance, a crime show's dialogue with what you have to say. This can cause trouble. Before telling them anything, ensure there is silence in the room. If there is traffic outside, shut the windows. Turn off the television, vacuum cleaner, or mixer. If they are watching a show or listening to music, gently ask them if you can turn it off for a minute so that you can talk to them. If they approach you to say something, stop the task at hand and give them complete attention. If they appear uncomfortable in a public place, give them earplugs. If it doesn't help, take them out of the space. Parks and beaches during quiet hours can be better alternatives.

Use Names

Call them by their official name or the one you

commonly use, for instance, father, while addressing them. If they do not recognize you, introduce yourself before proceeding: for example, "Hi, Mom, it's Brenda." Avoid nicknames such as honey, babe, and the like if they constantly have trouble recognizing you. Poor eyesight can also be the culprit. Ensure proper light in the room and help them wear their spectacles before moving further. When you introduce yourself, it can create a friendly atmosphere. Tell them your relationship with them ("I'm your daughter") only if you feel they still haven't recognized you. While conversing, say their name more than once to ensure they do not lose attention. Name objects as much as possible, for instance, "Have a chair," while pointing toward it. At times friends and relatives think there is no use visiting the patient if they don't remember them. However, any company can make them feel loved. My mother would be happy and welcoming to anyone who visited, even if she didn't recognize them. She would talk to them about her past and share stories of my childhood days. Any conversation that makes them happy is good conversation.

Use Non-Verbal Cues

Non-verbal language includes posture, facial expressions, and gestures. Many caregivers are unaware of their importance when dealing with their loved ones with dementia. If used effectively, non-verbal cues can create a positive impact, making it easy for you to handle many situations. Inwardly, you might be dealing with a million issues or worries, but you cannot express them to the patient for their ease of living. They are already going through a lot. Before entering their room, remind yourself about this and give your best performance. There is nothing insincere about it though. You are just putting up a brave face in front of them, which can be easier some days than the rest. Always remain calm and composed while approaching them. Keep a smile on your face, relax your body muscles and maintain a cool posture. They might not understand your facial expressions per se, but if your body language is tense, your loved one might sense something is wrong. When you appear neutral, there won't be any confusion in their mind. Also, your body language must match your expressions. It can be more difficult for some to hide their emotions if they are tense. Make sure you compose yourself before interacting with them. If you can't, take a break and let someone else take your place for a while.

Meanwhile, observe their body language and facial expressions for cues about their current mood and condition. See if they have a relaxed posture or if they appear tense. If they are breathing fast, there might be something troubling them. Your next course of action will depend on it. If you are in a public park and they become stiff or tense as a dog approaches them, take them away from the area. If they run out of words, they might show their displeasure through gestures, such as banging their hand on the wall, kicking, or getting restless. Past traumatic experiences and general dislikes can help you put two and two together easily. Whenever in doubt, consult someone who knows about certain phases of the patient's life better, for instance, their parents, friends, or colleagues. Don't let them dwell on the unpleasant events of the past.

If you wish to have a conversation with them, approach them in an effective manner. Do not stand by the door or afar where you are not visible enough to them, or it might seem you are talking to someone else. Offer your loved one to sit. If they are already seated, take a chair in front of them but maintain a safe distance. Be at the same level as they are or below and maintain eye contact with your loved one while talking. This would make you look less intimidating. Do not stand cross-bodied while discussing serious matters as it would show you are against them. Avoid sudden movements or walking while having a conversation. Do not engage in anything else such as answering the phone, playing with an object, or tapping your foot while talking to them to maintain their attention and make them feel important and valued.

At an advanced stage of dementia, language skills get severely impaired, and people begin communicating less, often using gestures instead of words. If you think they are getting confused identifying objects, say the name and point toward it. Tell them their soup is on their right side and point toward it. Gestures are especially helpful for people having severe listening impairments. However, if they can hear properly, do not overuse gestures as they can be distracting or irritating to them.

You can also use visual communication cards if your loved one suffers from hearing issues, aphasia, or language-related problems. You can either purchase them online or make them home on white paper with a black marker. You can even find pictures online and get them printed and laminated. Write simple words in bold letters or create pictures. If they understand their mother tongue better, use that language on the cards. The patient can point to the yes/no on a card. You can make the cards activity-specific, such as for personal hygiene, emotions, body pain, activities, and so on. If you feel they are behaving strangely, show them a card and ask if they have pain in any of the mentioned body parts. If they point at the leg, that means their leg hurts. You can even add a pain scale level section at the bottom from numbers 1-5.

. . .

Paraverbal Communication

Paraverbal communication includes tone, pacing, and volume of speech. If used effectively, it can change the way information is perceived and responded to. Think about what you are going to say before approaching your loved one. Use a friendly and calm tone while speaking. High pitch can seem threatening, whereas talking too slow can go unnoticed. Maintain an even volume and pitch throughout. Also, do not use authoritative language and tone.

Frame simple sentences and be really slow and clear while talking. If they forget why they have to visit a doctor, tell them it is for a routine checkup instead of reminding them of the detailed, complicated story. While giving instructions, guide them to take the first step, wait for them to finish, and then move ahead. If you say everything at once, they can forget half of what you said and get confused and pressured. Dementia often impairs one's ability to multitask. You can begin a conversation by stating how you think they are feeling, such as, "You seem a bit tense today." Wait for their reaction before moving further. Some days are better than the rest and you can judge that if you look closely. As the disease progresses, they might take extra time to register words and make sense of them before looking for a response.

Avoid Overwhelming Questions

Ask simple questions with one-word answers if their communication skills are weak, such as, "Would you like to have tea?" It's even better to skip the "you" and rather tell them, "Let's have tea." Do not confuse them with too many choices at once, for instance, "What would you like to wear?" Because this would mean they have to think about several options at once. Instead, give them two options—"Do you want the blue shirt or the yellow shirt?"—and let them pick one. Don't use condescending or childlike language with them since it would hurt their sentiments. Your job is to make them feel better about themselves. Tell the visitors to avoid questions such as, "Do you remember me?", "What did you eat for breakfast?" or "Did you get a call from Jerry the other day?" If their short-term memory is affected, these details might be fuzzy in their mind and create confusion. Even if the patient tells you they took medicine when they haven't, they might not be lying. They might not remember if they did. Open-ended questions can be used as a memory exercise to channel their emotions rather than seeking facts. While showing them their wedding picture, instead of, "Do you remember your wedding day?" ask, "What do you think of your dress?"

Be Creative

Analyze the mood of your loved one and talk accordingly. Use light humor if they are in a good mood and can understand it. Sometimes, laughing at your own mistakes can make the atmosphere light. Just don't laugh at them. If they are anxious or afraid, talk in a reassuring tone. Use your experience to create a list of their favorite activities. Say what would make them happy. If they love cooking, involve them in conversations about food. If they do not understand what you're trying to say, rephrase the sentence. You can create visual diaries about their life's journey at the initial stages, which can help them remember later. Take the help of post-its, pictures, and art as means of expression. Use large fonts and prefer yellow paper and a black pen or marker for writing.

Use sensory aids, such as perfume or soothing music of the sea that brings back happy memories. If they love petrichor, take them to the garden after it rains. Give them their favorite lotions to apply. Music can help set the mood and can be both entertaining and therapeutic. If they cannot convey something verbally, they can use drawing. Visual cards are also available for people with dementia. You can find an appropriate picture on the internet to communicate, especially if they have hearing trouble. If your loved one gets paranoid when you are away, leave a note while going to take a bath to assure them you are in the house. Do not say goodbye, rather tell them you will be back after getting groceries.

Observe how they react to being touched. While some people appreciate physical touch such as a hug, others might take it the wrong way. You can touch the back of their hand as a matter of assurance and check how they react. Don't shy away from showing your emotions. It can make you feel connected with them. Do not talk inaudibly with someone else while the patient is around and noticing you as they might take it as a conspiracy against them. Instead, if you can, include them in the conversation.

Don't Interrupt

Listen more, talk less. Encourage them to speak and express themselves as much as they can. If they are stuck on a word, let them figure it out themselves. Even if you know what they are saying, let them finish. Organize talking sessions regularly to maintain and practice their language skills. If they are saying something, be attentive and respectful about their emotions. Analyze what they have told you means to them and what it is coming from. If you are unsure of what they meant, repeat their words to check if that is what they mean. Encourage them to say more for you to understand properly. Do not make guesses. Also, do not correct them even if you feel they are wrong. If they call a potato a tomato, let it be. They might ask the same question more than once. Repeat the answer as politely as before. Elders often have a limited set of stories they keep repeating to remember the past. Hear them every time with the same enthusiasm.

HANDLING CURVE BALLS

Loved ones often ask questions that are hard to respond to since honesty can be stress-provoking. Not only can complicated sentences be overwhelming for a person with dementia, but negative answers can also be distressful and agitating. If they have always been an excellent driver and insist on driving the car, refusing them right away can sound demeaning and disrespectful. If their doctor approves, let them drive a little in your presence. Keep them away from high-traffic zones. If the doctor does not allow it and your loved one is aware of being unwell, be honest and let the doctor write it on a prescription pad. Show it to the loved one if they insist on driving. If they are at an advanced stage and do not remember why they cannot drive it, pick one of the following ways:

- Hide their driving license and tell them you also got a ticket for not having it once. Tell your loved one they can drive next time when you find their license card.
- Hide the car keys and take a taxi or cab while going out with them. Tell them the car needs repairing.
- Disconnect the car's battery, take out its ignition cap, or hide the batteries of the key, so that the engine does not start.

- Park the car somewhere else instead of your driveway or garage.

Even though all this may sound mischievous and downright fraudulent behavior, it is in their best interest only. A person with dementia can have poor vision or trouble multitasking, such as looking in multiple directions before taking a turn. They might get confused between brakes and accelerators or panic in a critical situation. This can even be unsafe for others and legally wrong. You cannot accept everything they say because you know their condition better. Consider one of the five strategies while handling conversational curve balls—accept, distract, redirect, bend the truth, or lie.

Accept

As discussed earlier, dementia affects a person's taste buds and their likes and dislikes are likely to fluctuate, sometimes rapidly. You might prepare their favorite dish, but they might say they hate it. If their short-term memory is affected and they don't remember being a vegan for the past ten years, don't argue with them. Accept their argument and apologize for forgetting about it. Give them another option, if possible. If they are hallucinating about someone being in their room, acknowledge it since it is real for them and assure them you will deal with the situation as you help them out of the room.

Distract

If the patient has a short attention span, distraction can work easily. If your loved one insists on going back to their old hometown, tell them to finish their food first. Once it is done, give them their medicines and involve them in another activity so that they do not remember their hometown anymore. If they get irritated and tell you to go away while you are giving them medicine, take it away and begin setting their clothes in the cupboard. After a few minutes, try afresh.

You can also actually leave the room and come back in another outfit.

Redirect

If they feel like meeting their parents who are long dead, redirect their argument and ask them where they live, how the place is, and what the patient loves about their parents, among other questions. Let them visualize it and go back to their happy place. Focus on the feelings and not the facts. If they talk about the food their mother cooked, ask how it smelled rather than telling them to remember the recipe. Analyze from their answer what they remember vividly and help them speak about it further.

Bend the Truth or Lie

The patient might either forget about someone passing or may deliberately be kept in the dark. At times, caregivers do not disclose if someone close to them has died. If they ask about such a relative, you can say they are fine or they are traveling and would come to meet them soon. If the doctor gives you some upsetting news about their deteriorating health, telling them about it can make it worse. Doctors often advise the carers to not share any traumatic news with the patient for their own safety. Lying for some is against their rules and is considered morally wrong. However, it can be used as a last resort if the truth would definitely cause them distress. You can even bend the truth by telling them the medicine is for their constipation instead of saying that the doctor changed their medication since it was causing the said side effect.

COMMUNICATING WITH THE MEDICAL TEAM

Help books and guides can give you ample knowledge but something will always be amiss. For those questions, there are doctors. Many times, it is the family doctor who notices dementia symptoms and suggests tests. If that is the case, you are liable to be confused. Be straight with the doctor and ask them anything you do not understand about the disease and its symptoms. If you have questions about other treatment options, ask them directly. Get information about the facilities available in their clinic or in the local area. Since they are the experts in this field, they can refer you to a good physiotherapist, dietician, and so on. Also, not everyone is an expert in deciphering the medical language of reports. Ask the doctor to explain technical jargon in simple terms. No question is silly. Doctors sometimes prescribe tests without telling why. But if you ask them, they would be helpful. Also, some medicines have multiple functions and side effects, and some symptoms can have multiple causes. You can ask those questions from the doctor. However, do not argue with the doctor about what you read online since there can be unverified or highly subjective information there. The doctor has the expertise, so try to not sound offensive based on speculations. Keep an open mind but be confident and relentless until all your questions have been addressed. If the doctor fails to satisfy you, you can find another doctor. But you won't know unless you ask.

Initially, your loved one would be the primary information source since they might have a better understanding of certain symptoms, such as bowel movements and body aches. Let them talk first and ask away their doubts and concerns. Let their voice be heard and ensure there is a minimum disturbance in the room so that they can talk freely. If you have any additional questions or feel they have missed out on something, get their permission before approaching the doctor.

Maintain a diary with minute details on the patient's daily behavioral changes, memory lags, and physical symptoms. Before the appointment, make a list based on the consistency of those symptoms since your last visit. People often forget half the things they had to ask by the time they meet the doctor. To avoid this, prepare a questionnaire and write pointers on a piece of paper or on your smartphone. If you change the doctor, take along all the reports and the complete list of medicines being administered. Also, share the previous ailments and treatment history with them. Do not downplay any symptoms. Even if it is just a recurring headache, tell them about it. Some symptoms may sound embarrassing for you to discuss openly but there is nothing the doctor hasn't already heard, so don't be shy. After the visit, if you still have doubts, call them up. You can write down the information you feel you will forget later. It is good to maintain a rapport with the medical team so that they are there for your guidance and assistance at any point. Even if you do not need them half as much now, the need will arise in the future.

6

HOME SAFETY

Being a caregiver is a lot of work, and making your home patient-friendly is one of the biggest challenges. Some of us live in ancestral houses, others in rented apartments. The house might be artistically made but still, require amends. Uneven surfaces and stairs can be hazardous. Even patterned tiles can be distracting for the patient. While solid color contrasts can be useful to distinguish objects, black and red must be used carefully since black can signify a hole and red cautionary. An all-white room can also be confusing for the patient, especially someone with vision problems. In some nations, professional services are available for renovations in the house as per the patient's symptomatic needs. Even if you don't have that facility in your area, you will find some tips ahead to make your life easy. Understand that your loved one is an independent person and might get offended if you are always assisting them in the house. You cannot be with them all the time either. To avoid accidents, these tips can come in handy. At some facilities physical restraints are also used to restrict the patient's movement, but they can do more harm than good if not handled well. You might not require all the changes in your house, half of them not at once either. Take a piece of paper and a pen; put yourself in the shoes of your loved one; evaluate every single room in the house based on their current symptoms and condition. Possible risk factors can be: wandering at night, trouble balancing, depth perception problems, spatial issues, poor vision, paranoia, a habit of rummaging through stuff, and trouble identifying objects and their usage.

PRACTICAL TIPS

While a carpeted floor is safer than tiles, tape regular carpets and mats all over the house to avoid skidding. You can also add childproof locks to cabinets in the kitchen, washroom, and laundry room. Install smoke alarms and gas detectors in your house. If the stairs are slippery, get them carpeted and add visible skid-proof tape at the edges. The railing must be sturdy. If needed, add a gate to the door to prevent them from using it unattended. Keep the rooftop door locked. Have proper light in the house and let the sunshine in during the day. Keep firearms, if any, hidden and properly locked. Install night lights at the spots they likely visit at night, such as the kitchen but keep the exit door out of sight. Write emergency call numbers near every phone in the house. Have the answering machine set to the minimum call option and lower the call volume so that it doesn't distract your loved one. Keep all the phones in the house at low volume and prevent the patient from falling prey to fraudulent harassing calls. If they get confused by a patterned wallpaper, replace it with a solid-colored one. Note down a list of similar tricks and hacks you can use. Do this every few months as per the disease advancement. However, only make changes in your house as your pocket allows. If your house has many red zones and you feel you cannot do much about it, consider renting another apartment or seek guidance from a physical or occupational therapist. Your loved one might not need several restrictions at once. At the advanced stage of dementia, you can hire a professional caretaker to be with them at all times or transfer them to a care facility where all the facilities are available.

BEDROOM
Have ample lighting in the room. If they have trouble walking, install a bell they can ring if they need anything. Have their room centrally heated or cooled. Do not attach portable appliances to plugs, which can be potentially harmful. Attach red tape around air vents as a sign of danger. Electric heating pads are safe options but do not charge them in front of the patient and keep the charging plug out of sight. Have a low-power bulb or nightlight in their room so that they do not have trouble finding the washroom at night. Have a waterproof bed protector in their room. Place a bed at an appropriate height and add a guardrail if they might roll off. If they often fall, keep hard and sharp-edged furniture away, such as a night dresser. You can also fix edge guards wherever possible. Keep a flashlight by their bed, and water and snacks in the room to avoid kitchen breaks at night. Remove the door lock for their safety. Properly cover the windows at night or have adequate light outside so that they are not scared of shadows. Cover or take out mirrors if they are perplexed or afraid of their reflection.

BATHROOM
Grab bars or handrails are helpful for the patient to avoid falling on the wet bathroom floor. Install them close to the

toilet seat, shower, and tub. Hand-held showers and a shower chair can be useful for the patient and caregivers in case the patient needs help bathing. If there are tiles in the washroom, you can attach skid-proof strips to the floor and have non-slip mats. If your loved one uses a bathtub, cover the faucet with a silicone cover as a precaution. To avoid scalding or freezing, fix the water temperature according to their preference. If you fear they might lock themselves in, get rid of it. The ideal situation is a washroom with no steps but if there are, help them every time they take a bath if they have a balancing issue. Their toilet seat must have a visible color. If not, use a fabric cover. Do not keep medicines in the cabinets. If they can take their medicines initially, give them a pill organizer with the time written on it instead of entire bottles. Keep a check and refill them after use. Keep minimal, usable items in the washroom. Use contrasting colors for different areas, if possible. Check the carpets and mats for wear and tear, fill cracks in the walls and floors, and change the batteries of appliances regularly. Take out the sliding door from the shower. If it has curtains, have tension rods installed. Replace the manual shaving kit with an electric shaver. If they have trouble using it, help them in the grooming process.

Living Room and Study Area

Keep the living room clean and clutter-free. Have minimal furniture for ease of walking. Do not keep too many showpieces in the living room and plants, if any, must not be toxic if consumed. Add window clings, stickers, or decals to avoid confusion. Cover the fireplaces or be careful while using them. Never leave the patient alone near an open, burning fireplace. Keep comfortable, sturdy chairs and couches with proper height and depth. Do not keep candles and incense sticks unattended. Avoid them if possible or keep them covered and out of the patient's reach. Hang family pictures on the wall they can relate to. Keep books inside cupboards with doors. Have a sturdy chair that does not rotate. If you have kids, pets, or both, their toys must be kept out of the way. There must not be hanging cords or glass objects in the living or study rooms. Keep your work-related laptop or computer away from your loved one or locked. Always have a backup for important documents.

Kitchen and Laundry Room

Add a safety nob on the gas stove or take it out altogether. Turn off the power source after use. Get appliances that turn off automatically. Take out stale food and trash regularly. Only keep safe food items on display, at eye level, either on the counter or in the refrigerator. Throw out any artificial object that can be mistaken for food. Keep unbreakable, colorful utensils in the kitchen and hide the rest behind locked cabinets. Color contrast can help the patient identify the food on the plate easily. Rotate solid utensil colors as per the dish. Have spoons with longer handles as they are easy to hold. Hide kitchen knives, matches, forks, scissors, plastic bags, and cleaning liquids if the patient doesn't remember how to use them. Hide all the unwanted appliances and disconnect the microwave wire after use. Use safety plugs to cover vacant sockets. Do not display alcohol bottles and tobacco items as they are not good for their health. Even an ashtray can remind them of it and a lighter can be dangerous in their hand. If it has a door, always keep the laundry room closed. Add child locks to cabinets containing detergents and other cleaning agents. Unplug the washing machine and dryer, or latch their doors after use. Keep ladders and stools out of the patient's reach to avoid falls.

GARAGE, BASEMENT, AND SHED

Keep all the mechanical tools, sports equipment, cleaning supplies, flammable chemicals, and ladders locked and hidden. If you do not have enough space to have cabinets, shut the doors and hide the keys. Always keep the vehicles locked and the keys out of reach. If you keep gym equipment in the basement, display only the safe items. Keep weights away. The basement can appear claustrophobic to some, so if your loved one seems uncomfortable being there, keep the door to it hidden. If they love driving, keep them away from the garage or cover up the vehicles.

EXIT AND EXTERIORS

Add motion sensors near the exit door. Hide the main door behind a curtain and keep the door knob less visible. Install deadbolts at the exit doors. As discussed before, keep a deep-colored round mat in front of the door with anti-slip tape. Before going to sleep, recheck if the exit doors are locked. Keep a spare key to the house with you or under the mat for your use if you are accidentally locked out. If your loved one uses a wheelchair or walker, build a railing by the door. If there is a railing already, install a handle for safe walking. Have textured tiles outside to prevent skidding. Keep the floor clean by hiding hoses, and taking out foliage, debris, leaves, ice, or water. Restrict the swimming pool area by covering it and installing a gate around it. Have fencing all around the house for safety. Keep the lawn well-maintained and lawn mower, grill, and fuels out of sight.

TECHNOLOGY

As toddlers need constant attention, people at an advanced stage of dementia also require ceaseless assistance, which is not possible for a sole person to handle efficiently all the time. If the patient has a habit of walking around, the caregiver is constantly paranoid and worried about their whereabouts, having trouble sleeping or doing household chores, let alone going out. People with dementia often mix up day and time. If they have a fixed schedule for medicine, they would either begin asking what time it is or wonder whether they took the medicine. After waking up at odd hours, sometimes they doubt whether it is daybreak already. They might also drift to an older time and then have trouble remembering people. For all these issues, gadgets can help. Over the past years, several technological advancements have been made to ease the life of patients and carers. Automatic pill dispensers, portable radios, talking picture albums, sensory blankets, toys, and other stimulators are available in the market. These tools can address potential threats and thus assist both the caregiver and patient in the right direction. A patient can have autonomy, independence, and a better quality of life while the caregiver can be less stressed out. You can keep an eye on your loved one even when you are not in their room and track them so that they do not get lost in the crowd. Before purchasing anything, check the price and customer reviews, and compare products as per your requirement. Ensure they are easy for you to operate on and are safe for patients with dementia.

Clocks

A clock in their room and other areas can reduce the patient's stress and paranoia about keeping time. They can effectively manage their schedule without asking the caregiver repeatedly and being suspicious of the answer they get each time. The basic questions in the patient's mind are whether it is day or night, and what day, date, month, or year it is. Disorientation often begins at a middle stage and since the patient is aware of their forgetfulness, they feel reluctant to ask. Modern-day clocks can solve their problem effectively. You can hang them at their eye level in their bedroom and living room.

Day clocks are simplistic and have names of the days on them, written in a huge and clear font. Some of these also mention if it is morning, noon, or evening. The patient can check if it is a weekend or a working day and if it is the time to sleep, as you told them. They come both in manual analog and digital formats. The digital ones, also called calendar clocks, mention the time along with the date. Some of them even have audio features, so if the patient does not remember how to check time anymore, digital clocks can be helpful. With a digital clock, you can change font settings and language using a remote, which is convenient for those whose short-term memory falters. They can also be kept anywhere in the house and can be programmed to set detailed alarms, such as with a display or sound of medicine time. Through voice-control technology, reminders can be set in a custom voice or play a recorded message in your loved one's voice. As opposed to analog clocks, digital clocks are available in many forms and with different features and rates, which you can choose as per your needs. With this facility, patients can utilize their timetable effectively, watch their favorite shows, and take medicines on time. Moreover, virtual assistant technology is quickly gaining traction these days and it is a fun way to communicate. Even elders enjoy talking to a customized virtual voice such as Alexa and asking for time, weather forecasts, and any other questions anywhere in the house. A talking button clock is another simple tool that tells time every time you push a circular button. You can also download applications and widgets on their digital devices if your loved one still uses them.

Communication Aids

Since mobile phones have become an inevitable part of our lives today, initially, it is necessary to make simple changes, such as keeping only essential contact numbers with pictures on the phone, adding or updating emergency contact numbers, and installing simpler applications, voice assistance, and widgets for daily use. Social media and video calling services like FaceTime, Zoom, Skype, etc., make people feel connected. Spam and fraudulent calls and accounts must be blocked on all devices and incoming and outgoing calls regularly monitored since people with dementia are prone to be duped by miscreants. Meanwhile, a smartphone can become seemingly complicated with time. A landline can be the second best option, especially for elders. For people with trouble remembering phone numbers, you can keep instructions close, probably pasted on the wall. There are even simple cell phones and landlines with speed dial and adaptive technology. If their eyesight fails, they can purchase phones with a large dial pad. Other phones have customized pictures with pre-programmed numbers instead of dial-pad or caption-enabled phones to pick up voice and turn it into text version.

Electrical Appliance Monitoring

Electrical appliances can be hazardous to use without supervision. They can cause electric shock, fire, and burns if not used properly. Use a wall outlet or power strip that alerts the caregiver of the appliance being turned on or off. Their main function is to detect a power outage and protect appliances from damage. Inexpensive power strips are available on the market, and you can control these with a remote. Some of them also have motion sensors, which turn the appliances off when no one is around. Most of them contain a power switch. Get it checked and replaced every 24 months or so. If your loved one is alone in the house, you can still monitor them through their appliance usage and if they do not use anything the entire day, you can check if anything is wrong with them and send help.

GPS LOCATION AND TRACKING DEVICES

There are multiple wearable tracking devices and alarm systems available in the market. Let your loved one have more than one of these devices at a time while going out so that if something is misplaced, you can utilize the other one. For instance, mobile phones can fall off people's hands or pockets. They can also forget to take them along. In such cases, other options can prove helpful. Tracking devices use geo-fencing technology, which can be programmed to create a virtual boundary wall. If the patient crosses it, the device will notify you. Your loved one can thus safely go out for a walk alone if they prefer. These devices often have speaker, and hearing features. There are panic alarms too, which have a single button, through which the patient can contact you in an emergency. There are smart wristwatches, clothing tags, pendants, and other products available for daily use with GPS location tracking technology. A SmartSole can be placed in the footwear itself. Many major companies have come up today, offering tracking services, such as AngelSense, Apple, iTraq, and so on. Find the most effective and affordable ones as per your need.

Home Monitoring Devices

Motion detectors that use infrared energy can be used in key areas, especially the ones that light up or send a discrete signal and do not blare horns that scare the patient. If they cross those places, such as the back door, you will be notified immediately. Some alarms also facilitate the carer to talk to their loved one for assistance. You can also purchase carpets, and window and door sensors. Cameras and voice recorders can be installed in their room and other locations at an advanced stage. They can be set at angles so that they have their privacy but you can check their well-being. If you have a professional caretaker at home, you can monitor everything through the camera as an added safety measure. Video doorbells can add another safety feature to the house. You can even have an outdoor camera to check the direction where your loved one went or who entered the house. Baby monitors can be installed in their bedroom so that you can hear a call for help. Home care robots are also innovative in the sense they can charge themselves and need no outer assistance to function. Once programmed, they can clean the house, set reminders, and alert others in case of an emergency. They can even be used for robotic pet therapy as they can interact with the patient, keep them company, and thereby reduce their stress and anxiety. Today, common appliances such as a refrigerator or microwaves also have a camera facility and an added microphone system. Other features of smart devices include fall sensors, and panic alarms that monitor the patient's heart rate, blood pressure, and other vital functions. These work on Personal Emergency Response Systems (PERS), and can sound medical emergency alerts in critical situations either outdoors or inside the house, at any given time.

7

LEGAL, FINANCIAL, AND HOUSING MATTERS

Life expectancy in the case of dementia varies from 2 years to 25 years on average, depending on the diagnosis and subtype. There are methods to delay the symptoms but there is no telling how the body would react to different medicines and treatment plans. People diagnosed with dementia often begin worrying early and rightly so about their future in terms of their savings, treatment plan and expenditure, and major decisions related to their health, living arrangements, and property. For all those burning questions, assistance is available. When the patient still has the authority over their mind, they can make valuable decisions in a living will and pass future decision-making authority to someone they trust, most probably their caretaker. It is an emotional phase in the patient's life as much as it is for the caretaker. It is a huge responsibility to take life and death decisions for someone you love. Be sure your loved one gives this authority willingly when they can, as per their wish.

Effective estate planning takes care of all your decisions while living and after death. However, such a plan does not immediately nullify your loved one's authority. It comes into effect when the patient can no longer decide for themselves. The caregiver must let the person with dementia decide for themselves for as long as they can. If they do not reply well during one part of the day, try again when they are in a better condition. If they take time to decide, have patience. If they have forgotten important information, help them remember using cues. Memory comes and goes, but the decision-making skills are not lost as early in the case of dementia. A person can have more than one representative to handle different matters and decide on a substitute in case the first one fails to fulfill their duty. If the patient does not make this decision on time, then the court has the authority to appoint a surrogate for medical decisions and a conservator for monetary decisions. These people are mostly selected from the patient's immediate family and might not be as per the patient's wishes. If no family member is selected, the state hires its own representative to take important decisions.

Some documents do not need professional help but for others, your loved one must hire a lawyer. The patient can take the help of their friends, area aging agencies, bar associations, legal aid offices, social workers, non-profit organizations, or government officials to find a suitable attorney. Check out the directory of the National Academy of Elder Law Attorneys and lawhelp.org for options. Share a copy of the prepared documents with their doctor. Your loved one can keep the legal documents in a safe place but tell someone they trust about the location. Meanwhile, everything needs not to be updated in the document. Once a person has been given the authority, the patient can share their further wishes with them verbally. The patient must be open with other family members about their decisions so that there are no conflicts later. Another important aspect is health insurance benefits, which can ease the financial burden on the patient and their family. We shall discuss these aspects at length ahead.

HEALTH CARE

Since by now the patient knows the common symptoms of their disease and possible complications coming their way in the future, they can decide what they are comfortable with. From being admitted to the hospital to being kept on life support, all the decisions can be in the hands of the patient early on, provided they are clinically competent. It means they can gain information, make decisions based on it, and communicate those decisions effectively to the court. The decision-making power of the patient can vary at different durations, and it is taken into consideration. The doctor is supposed to share a list of possible interventions based on their study and other patients' treatment history. The decisions made by the patient must also be autonomous, without anyone's influence or pressure. If the patient is not considered fit by the court to make their own decisions, then the court can appoint a surrogate. A surrogate is generally a family member who knows about their preferences regarding the treatment plan, such as their choice to go peacefully rather than living a vegetative life. Also, though some people welcome the idea of organ donation, others are likely to refuse due to cultural and religious contexts. Government standards and ways of determining competency may vary from place to place, so the patient must get legal help as soon as they can. There are two kinds of medical formalities.

Living Will

A living will is a guideline, not a legal document, prepared by the person with dementia and contains decisions related to current and possible future health conditions. This document mentions previous ailments and preferred doctors with their contact details. A person can have a family dentist or physiotherapist whose services they would like to continue. It also contains critical decisions, for example, what to do in case they are in an artificial life support system. One can mention all their preferences for end-of-life here. Some other major choices include whether or not to allow intubation, resuscitation, or organ donation for research or transplantation. It also contains their preference for medical care facilities, if needed toward the final stage. The patient can also decide well in advance if they would like to die in the hospital or home, and if they want any other facility, such as the company of friends. Some demands are related to their culture. Discussing possible situations can be a traumatic experience but having no power over such situations later can be worse. Through this document, their practitioner can make quick and informed decisions.

DURABLE POWER OF ATTORNEY

This piece of paper or advance directive transfers medical decision-making power to someone else, if they no longer can, themselves. This person, named as a proxy, power of attorney, representative, or agent, has to be consulted if the 'living will' falls short. Some situations are not anticipated by the patient while making a living will, such as sudden accidents. Also, sometimes the patient's mentioned choices are subjective and require interpretation. Also, the proxy can hire or change the patient's doctor, enroll them in other treatment plans, or hire a healthcare worker. On a personal level, your loved one can share their likes and dislikes for effective home care, their fears and past experiences, a list of people they would like to keep in contact with, and their eating, grooming, and personal hygiene habits. If you find yourself in a fix on a decision, seek guidance from past experiences, their value system, and others close to them. Have their best interests at heart, including their physical, emotional, and mental well-being, and weigh the pros and cons accordingly.

FINANCIAL DECISIONS

Many nations are emphasizing that their citizens create a will early in life and update it regularly. A person's will contains information about the distribution of their money, property, and other valuables to beneficiaries of their choice. It also includes decisions and investments in their funeral and burial arrangements. However, this will is only read and followed after the person's death. For decisions when alive, a living trust has to be created. If the patient does not hire a substitute to make official financial decisions for them in time, a family member or primary carer can take up the role voluntarily; though this process then becomes complicated, costly, and time-consuming. The patient can hire a healthcare representative for this purpose as well or someone with financial expertise. Some people even hire a trust for the purpose. People with dementia can get financial help through a Medicare card if they are above sixty-five years old or more, or have a disability. Medicaid is available for families with low-income. A person can use both cards at once to get maximum benefit. These can cover the cost of tests, prescriptive medicines, and hospice facilities. For nursing care or homebound treatment, the days covered are limited.

. . .

LIVING TRUST

A designated trustee, also called the executor, manages the living trust and designates funds as per the patient's wishes before and after their death. This executor can even be their bank instead of a family member. This includes paying for their attorney, loans, mortgages, insurance policies, taxes, pension plans, and registered retirement savings plans (RRSPs). An insurance policy can be for an automobile, house, life, or disability. They also manage their investments such as their house, vehicle, or business. Their priority is to cater to the needs of the patient, followed by their dependents if any. People with dementia must ensure all their financial liabilities are handled appropriately. They can either sell off assets they no longer need or transfer ownership to someone they trust. Some people get support from their workplace initially and continue with their job. If they own a business, they can have a second-in-command and prepare all the legal documents for a smooth transition after they retire.

DURABLE POWER OF ATTORNEY

This is the person selected to make financial and legal decisions after the patient is declared unfit to do so. The patient can share their priority list in terms of finances to maintain the standard of living they seek. They might wish to continue their meditation classes, prefer a certain kind of food, or allocate a part of their money for a dependent's education. Handling this duty begins when the patient can no longer handle money or gets paranoid about making mistakes in calculation. Letting them carry on this task can increase aggression and suspicion. Also, they can make incorrect transactions, get duped, or lose their cards. A durable power of attorney can manage their money and give them small amounts of money they can easily handle. If the patient chooses to live alone initially, the attorney can pay their bills and assist in purchasing household items.

LONG-TERM CARE FACILITIES

Though you might wish to be personally available for your loved one at every step of the disease, there is no harm in knowing your options for outside assistance. In fact, keeping this option open can be an effective step toward end-of-life planning. For some people, it might be unacceptable to abandon their loved one like that but toward the end, their situation can take an unexpected turn. At that point, you might not get enough time to make an informed choice. Discuss this with your loved one and make a list of available options around you. You can even visit some of them and check their arrangements, facilities, and staff members.

At the intermediate stage, you can hire an in-house professional for temporary or full-time assistance to provide personalized care in the luxury of their house such as preparing meals, giving medication, and personal attention. This facility can be costly, however, and everyone might not be satisfied with the services provided. So it is better to prepare in advance and keep a list handy. If you ever feel it is getting difficult to manage alone, you can use these numbers in any order you prefer until satisfied. In some cases, hallucinations and paranoia get out of hand and there are repeated cases of aggression. This can be a cause behind seeking the help of a healthcare center. Sometimes the elders themselves prefer these facilities for future care. At an advanced stage of dementia, the patient needs extra care. The patient might be unable to perform any task, such as swallowing food, taking medicine, walking, or responding to others. They might even require consistent medical assistance due to incontinence, lack of nutrition and immunity, and other factors. Even an infection can cause pneumonia, which can be fatal for the patient. For a caregiver, this can be a traumatizing and overwhelming situation to witness. So even if you never wish to send them to a healthcare facility, it is better to make an informed decision than an uninformed one. Gaining knowledge can help you gain peace of mind and make better health-related and financial plans. There are both government-funded and private healthcare units all around.

Long-term facilities include nursing homes, assisted living, and residential facilities. At whichever stage you seek professional help, consider that your options can vary according to the patient's symptoms and can be narrowed down based on an assessment of cognitive skills, behavioral alterations, and other aspects, together being called activities of daily living (ADLs). You can take your loved one with dementia along so that they have a say about it. Some patients specifically write in their living will that they must not be admitted to a particular facility. Instead of being burdened with this decision alone, it is better to let them decide. You can get information on this at your local Alzheimer's Association or Long-Term Ombudsman offices. Shortlist the places you would like to visit and arrange meetings with their administrators. Once there, enquire about their facilities and care approaches, including the level of involvement in the patient's care. Meet the staff members, and check out the list of activities, additional costs, and hospice waivers offered by them. Another thing to know is if the family and friends are allowed in the facility and how you can play a role in their care along with the staff members. Note that some organizations have stricter rules on this than the rest. Furthermore, enquire about their racial, religious, ethnic, and cultural inclusiveness. You can also inspect the rooms and safety measures, talk to the patients, and visit their eating section. Some places were badly affected by the COVID-19 pandemic and faced acute staff shortages and poor conditions, so be mindful and check their current situation before deciding. You must also know beforehand about the rules on visiting the patient so that there is no confusion later on. Remember that healthcare cards do not cover all the cost of healthcare facilities. Read their offer agreements carefully. Some of the possible housing facilities are listed below.

Assisted Retirement Housing Facility

A retirement housing facility can be entirely independent or provide basic assistance to elders. An assisted retirement room, apartment, or condo is a safe space for people with various issues such as cardiovascular disease, depression, etc. Also known as a Care Home, it is suitable for people in the initial dementia stage. Some facilities even have a dedicated Alzheimer's unit, for instance. It still offers more independence to the individual than a nursing home and there is limited interference. Healthcare workers are available for patients at an added price who cater to their daily medical, recreational, cognitive, personal care, and health requirements, though no one is assigned for a particular patient at all times. Staff members can help them dress up, prepare food, and give medicine on time. The facilities offered may vary, along with the cost as per the area and additional needs, so it is better to get more details before signing up. Some of them even have a golf court, swimming pool, book club, fitness center, and so on. Individuals or couples can choose this facility for independent dwelling. One can also get transportation facilities. Another retirement facility is Continuing

Care Retirement Community (CCRC), wherein a person can live independently at first and, as the disease progresses, shift to higher levels of assistance. As per Genworth's national cost of care survey, an assisted living facility has a monthly median cost of $4,635 in 2022, which was $135 more than that of 2021. This cost is not covered by the Medicare card.

Group Home

A group home is a more economical and homely option as opposed to an assisted retirement house. It appears like a regular house where people with similar needs live together and are assisted by one or more trained staff members. Often the patient-staff ratio is optimum. Home-cooked, personalized meals are available here and there can be 10-20 people in a single home, though this value varies state-wise. Some of these homes even allow pets. Most facilities even provide transportation services, but you must confirm it before making any commitment. Their cost varies from $3,500 to $10,000 per month. Medicaid and long-term insurance can cover their cost. Since group homes provide support to people from different walks of life, such as people with disabilities, orphans, or those having faced substance abuse, you must enquire if the one you visit can cater to your needs and whether it is authorized to do so. Unlike assisted houses, they might not have a market for daily needs nearby and unlike a nursing center, they do not provide medical facilities.

Specialized Nursing Center

Such a center is a part of a building that is federal-government-regulated. Some facilities are also Medicare-certified. A nursing center is meant for people at an advanced level of dementia and offers round-the-clock surveillance, physical, medical, and recreational facilities, diet plans to provide proper nutrition, spiritual and meditation rooms, and a dedicated health official for each patient. They also offer occupational and speech therapies. From treatment of wounds to ventilator support, a wide range of services are available here under one roof. They do accept Medicare cards and cover some of the additional costs. A private room can have a median value of $9,305 and a semi-private room can have $8,145 of it per month (Genworth's survey for 2022).

Memory Care Unit

Such a facility is specifically designed to assist patients at an advanced level with a particular kind of dementia. The security level might vary though it is aimed at providing a secure space where patients are monitored to avoid them getting lost. gadgets such as tracking bracelets, alarm doors, secure elevators, and so on are a part of their security system. Activities related to cognition, behavior, socializing, and so on are available with highly trained staff. Its cost is just below $7,000 per month on average, depending on the level of assistance required and the area.

The main issue behind dementia care is its collective cost that everyone cannot afford since a large chunk of patients belong to low and middle-income categories. Also, medical cards can be used for short-term and not long-term treatments. The first step toward creating a durable plan to manage finances is creating a list of assets, income sources, and other expenses. You can download the PDF file on the official website of an NGO named Alzheimer's Association. Have a discussion about the available funds with your trusted family members and see if anyone can offer further support. Seek help from financial and legal advisers once you have the list. Calculate dementia care plan expenses, which must include the treatment cost, apartment modification cost, charges of paid caregivers, and care facilities. Check government policies, retirement benefits, insurance cover offers, community support services, respite care, and medical cards. All this would give you a rough estimate of your situation and the budget you can allocate for different services and the expenses you can cut down on, such as installing expensive gadgets in the house. Make a priority list and set some money aside for emergencies.

8

CAREGIVER WELLNESS

I might have left this discussion for the last, but it is as essential as the rest of the planning to be a successful caregiver. Your role throughout your loved one's journey with dementia is to be their strength and hope to fulfill their desires and honor their will. However, most caregivers take it as a burden upon themselves and forget themselves while taking care of the patient. Others constantly feel guilty about not doing enough, blaming themselves for everything gone wrong, and pushing themselves to their limit before realizing they are drowning themselves. To stay afloat, you need rest, help, and maybe some ice cream. And no, seeking help would not prove you are inadequate. It only proves you are human. If you change yourself entirely while taking care of a person with dementia, you will be lost once they are gone.

As per several studies, in America, most caregivers are women taking care of their parents or spouse and it takes a great toll on their health. Based on cultural values, financial situation, and family support available, the burden on caregivers varies. Some cultures look down upon sending their loved ones to a care home and prefer doing everything themselves. Others do not have enough finances to get outside help or family support to seek unpaid assistance. Many caregivers either work less or leave their jobs and since the entire treatment is not covered under government schemes, lose their savings to pay for their loved one's treatment. Often in this, their own health gets neglected. Most of the caregivers report being burdened physically, emotionally, and financially over the course of treatment. Osteoporosis, diabetes, anxiety, depression, insomnia, heart diseases, and other chronic illnesses are reported higher among caregivers of dementia than the rest. They also have a loss of social life since they cannot leave their loved ones alone. For many, even a care home does not ease the burden because they feel obliged to take care of their maximum requirements and toward the end of life, the caregivers are constantly on their toes, getting no rest at all. There is no dearth of cases where the caregiver died soon after or before the patient. COVID-19 made the situation worse since social life was further severed, medical help was hard to get, and workplaces shut down completely. Caregivers were exhausted and overburdened, and the fear of the disease was as bad as its effect on those lacking immunity.

What usually keeps a caregiver going on is their love for the person, a sense of duty toward them, spiritual fulfillment, traditional values, personal growth, returning the favor, social pressure, and in some cases, lack of choice. Whatever the reason, it is essential to note that self-care for a caregiver is not a luxury, but a necessity. It is a survival mechanism to take out some time, even if a few minutes, out of your routine every day for your needs. Here are some of the tips to begin taking small steps to improve your physical health.

- **Make a proper routine.** Ditch alcohol and caffeine at night so that you can sleep well. Your loved one will not wake up at night if they have a hectic day, so you don't need to worry too much. You need rest too. Try other relaxation techniques than getting addicted to sleeping pills.

- **Meditation** can help calm down your nerves. Even if you get 5 minutes to do this, close your eyes and concentrate. Sit straight, cross-legged on the floor, and keep your hands on your knees. Breathe in as deeply as you can through your stomach and then breathe out. It will relax your mind and release stress.

- **Step out of the house in natural light**, even if merely to the balcony. Go out for a walk and listen to music for a while if you have no company. Stretch your muscles to release tension. A 30-minute workout is enough every day, but you can begin by sparing at least 10 minutes for it.

- **Maintain a self-care diary and set alarms for yourself on your smartphone.** Don't neglect yourself. Since your loved one needs proper nutrition, change your eating habits as well. However, customize your diet chart according to your needs and not to match your loved one's. If red meat is recommended for you, have it.

- **Do not skip meals or eat in a hurry.** Involve your loved one in the cooking process to make it a fun activity but if you do not like to cook, hire someone. You can even get the food delivered if you lack motivation on a particular day.

- **Get regular check-ups and take your medicines** or over-the-counter dietary supplements timely. Some medicines have a complete course, and if left midway they can cause side effects, so do not stop any prescription medicine without the doctor's consent.

- **Do not handle everything alone.** Ask family, friends, and other people you trust for help from time to time. Hire a professional healthcare worker. If you have doubts about whether they would manage well, check reviews before hiring. Create a team you can count on. You can also avail of adult daycare services to take time out for yourself.

- **Break the old traditions in the house.** Even if you host a grand Christmas party every year, you can let it rest if you do not have the energy to make all those preparations. People who love you will understand. Have as much on your plate as you can comfortably manage.

- **Make it a rule to get consistent and regular breaks from caregiving.** Use this time to relax. If you don't feel like meeting others, sit in a park by yourself for an hour reading a book you love. If you feel exhausted, don't push yourself. Take a nap to rejuvenate yourself.

- **Use activities meant for your loved one for your benefit**, for instance, plant vegetables with them if you find it therapeutic. Listen to music, dance, or watch a comedy movie with them. Build good memories that you can cherish long after they are gone.

Some of the home care facilities are covered by Medicaid, Medicare, and private insurance plans. Get information and make an effective plan. Also, there are several caregiver support groups available online and in-person. Find the ones related to dementia. Even if you do not feel like sharing your story with anyone, you can listen to others' experiences and get insights. There may be something others know more, or they might have a way of coping that works for you as well. Remember, self-care is for self-preservation. You have to manage your routine around theirs. If you are well-rested and fit, you can manage your daily tasks more efficiently rather than being stressed. You will have more patience and mental capacity to handle difficult situations. So even while you are thinking about your requirements, you are not being selfish. Stay open to challenges and be flexible but do not neglect your physical health.

COPING WITH EMOTIONS

Once you have made a plan to ensure physical well-being, another challenge in front of you is dealing with your mental health. Caregiving is already a difficult task but when emotional stress adds to it, the situation gets worse. A perfect day can suddenly become emotionally charged if the person with dementia gets angry, frustrated, or aggressive over something. It can sometimes appear like a thankless job, with your loved one getting angry at you and being hurtful in their conduct. Ask yourself if it was really about you. As discussed before, their reality is different from yours. So do not argue with them as it can escalate things. Once you have mastered the art of effective conversation, you know when it is dementia speaking and not your spouse or parent. But can you really ignore all they say? Even if you do, many caregivers feel helpless watching such a huge transition in their loved one's personality. It sometimes takes up all the efforts of a person to appear neutral, calm, and relaxed when on the inside, they are traumatized. Thinking the conversation through before actually saying something can also be difficult and one is bound to make mistakes once in a while. You might not have a solution to everything, and it is okay to feel confused sometimes. If the spouse has dementia, the caregiver is more likely to feel helpless and alone due to lost intimacy and emotional support. While some caregivers remain content with the intimacy they share with their partner, others find it very frustrating and feel like they no longer feel emotionally connected with them, almost as if they are living with a stranger.

Seeking timely help is necessary because chronic stress and its effects can seep in unannounced. The common red flags that show you need help are losing hope, being unable to concentrate on the tasks you once loved, overthinking, blaming yourself, feeling emotionally drained and irritable, being negative, preferring to stay alone, having suicidal thoughts, tiredness, body pain, regular headaches, and sudden weight gain or loss. If untreated, they can make your life horrible. While opening up with a person of trust is the best option to acknowledge the issue, a journal can also help. You can write down all your emotions on it. Though it is okay to vent sometimes, you have to move past this point.

Since you cannot change the behavior of the other person or reason with them, it is best to accept it and be proud that you put in the effort and continue to do so despite the hurdles.

Make small changes in your daily routine to stay active and mentally fit. Take your time in the bathroom. Brush your teeth, take a bath, and wash your hair regularly as you did before. Dressing up can also appear difficult when you are stressed out. Even if you are not going anywhere, make a little effort to dress nicely. Wear comfortable clothes yet something that makes you feel good about yourself. If there is too much furor throughout the day in your house, wake up a little early to have your tea or coffee in peace. Sit in a comfortable chair outside and appreciate the nature around you before beginning the routine. Notice the birds and the squirrels around. Buy something for yourself. It can be a new moisturizer or a mobile phone cover. It doesn't have to be costly. Shopping is also considered a great stress buster. It stimulates our senses and signifies a sense of control over our situation and circumstances. A common sign of depression is lacking the motivation to finish household chores such as washing clothes or cleaning the rooms. Push yourself out of bed if that happens. We have discussed before why a tidy house is essential. Involve other family members in the process. Play music while washing dishes or folding clothes.

Don't stop socializing if you have good friends. If you feel they can't understand you or undermine your situation, speak up. Don't let anyone put you down. Have a circle of people around who uplift your spirit in times of distress and genuinely care for you. Interact with other caregivers through online communities and local support groups. Many communities are specifically to discuss a particular type of dementia and contain valuable information and practical tips for common problems. Many members with expertise and experience can guide you. You can either share your emotions or hear out from others. It can help you feel connected and form a sense of kinship with other caregivers. You can even create a guide you can refer to whenever in doubt. If you constantly feel demotivated, practice positive self-talk by writing down the following sentences in your journal:

- I am doing whatever I can to the best of my ability.
- The situation I am in would be hard for anyone to deal with.
- I am not perfect but to err is human.
- Everything is not in my control.
- Every mistake is a learning experience, and every day is a chance to improve.
- Sometimes, I just need to focus on short-term goals.
- I will rejoice in the current moments rather than worry about the future.
- Dementia is to be blamed for their anger and distress and not something I did.
- I will try to get professional help if caregiving takes a toll on my health.

Whenever you feel exhausted, go back to look at these sentences. You can add anything else that you have in mind to the list. Another technique is to close your eyes and visualize yourself in a serene and happy place. You can also learn yoga, and tai chi, or get a relaxing therapy to release muscle tension. If this does not help, follow the last point and seek medical help. Mental health professionals such as therapists and social workers can help you through the emotional toll that caregiving can bring. Many insurance providers cover some of the costs.

REWARDS OF CAREGIVING

Emotionally, the years of caregiving are like a long rollercoaster ride for everyone, though personal experiences vary. Some people get too exhausted toward the end that death comes as a relief. Those who get more support and take care of their mental and physical well-being are comparatively less burnt out. If a proper plan is made and followed, the journey can be pleasant for a large part of the patient's life. It will also be less of a burden on you. Exceptions are always there since the core values and habits of a person also vary. Your loved one might have always been a calm person or a fussy eater. A person I knew had always been a foodie. As dementia progressed, his demands for specific foods rose and he always wondered when they were eating again. For a caregiver, this experience has some re-affirming rewards too. For one, it gives people a purpose in life. It is a long-term commitment that demands education, resources, time, and effort. You wake up with a purpose every day and prepare an itinerary for the day. You learn a lot about your state's healthcare system while caring for your loved one and get to interact with healthcare and social care experts.

While maintaining your loved one's social life, you inadvertently build your own as well, learning empathy and patience from other caregivers. Even if you have been modest and underestimated yourself all along, you get an appreciation for your efforts in these settings as new caregivers ask your opinion or look up to you for guidance. People with dementia also often are dependent on their primary caregivers and follow them everywhere. They might shout at you once in a while, but that can't neglect the fact that they have put their faith in you, thus giving you the power to make valuable decisions for them. It's an achievement in itself to be trusted by someone like that. When all this ends and you have fulfilled their wishes and given them a farewell they desired, it will be an accomplishment on your part.

In terms of relationships, there is no doubt you will see major changes. The people you believed were the best for you would disappear in a puff of smoke. But then you will find that the ones you always underestimated stand by you in the toughest of times. You will also find new friends and acquaintances along the way. At your home also, you would have a sense of comradeship as everyone will be working toward the same goal, that is, taking care of your loved one, they key to which is effective communication and problem-solving skills. Your children, if any, would watch you and learn. You can become a role model for them and also for others in your family and friend circle.

CONCLUSION

Success for a caregiver is all about seeing your loved one go peacefully, after having lived a life they always wanted. But there are high chances you wouldn't realize it now when they are still there. All you see now is a changed person, fighting a war they cannot win. But there is a fighter inside them, and so is in you; that is why you purchased this book in the first place. With your new-gained knowledge, create a detailed plan after consulting your trusted doctor. If you are noticing dementia-like symptoms in someone, don't make assumptions and get the tests done. Once you receive the diagnosis report, give yourself time to process the information and decide the next course of action. Prepare a list of questions you have in mind and be open with your doctor about them. The doctor cannot tell you how many years your loved one has since it is based on a lot of factors that pan out in the future. Older individuals usually have less life expectancy than younger ones. Effective caregiving has been scientifically proven to affect longevity and quality of life. Remember, your loved one can have more than one type of dementia and if they are your parents, you might have it too in the future. So if you have hypertension, diabetes, high cholesterol, or blood pressure, start taking your health seriously now while you are handling your parents' medicinal and dietary needs. Check preventative measures and implement them. Ensure your loved one has all the legal formalities handled. Check financial aid available for them and make an estimated budget. Be it alternate treatment, social group, memory cafe, or a nursing center, be their eyes and ears and make informed choices. Talk to administrators, ask volunteers, check reviews, and make visits. Check out the best options nearby for cognitive stimulation, occupational, speech, and language therapies, and physiotherapy if they are not available inside the doctor's clinic. Enroll them in groups related to their favorite activity. Decide their place of residence and make the necessary renovations. Install gadgets that can ease your worries. Discuss with your family members about your treatment plan and give them information either verbally or by sharing resource material from time to time. Instead of giving updates to every individual separately, you can form a common group with core members in it to build a strong team. Avoid conflicts as they can take up a large part of your mental space. And when the time comes, honor their last wishes so that they go peacefully.

Most importantly, breathe. You do not have to become a perfect caregiver overnight. It is a process and thankfully, you still have time. Use this time efficiently to be prepared for the challenges ahead. Be realistic and practical about it because that is the only way forward. If you live in denial or fail to adapt to the changing situation, there will be management issues and it will cause trauma to both you and your loved one. Use the tips given in the book to manage your emotions and channel them. While you are working on your personal goal to give the best possible treatment to your loved one, your country is not behind either. Research work is continuing in this field by government and voluntary organizations. In America, the National Alzheimer's Project Act (NAPA) was established on January 4, 2011, by then-president Barack Obama to streamline research work to find better medicines and a cure for dementia. Efforts are also on to ensure early diagnosis of the disease, provide help to the minorities, and financial aid to people with low income. Governments all over the world are also dedicated to educating people about dementia so that their perspective changes and they become more accommodating. There are laws in place to prevent fraud and scams against people with dementia. Steps are also being taken to hire more healthcare workers everywhere to provide individual attention to patients. Besides, several voluntary organizations throughout America are catered to raising funds for research work and guidance. Many of them have support groups that you can join either virtually or in person. Some of them even offer tips on lifestyle changes to prevent dementia. Steps are on to bring the public and private sectors together to form coordination and coherence.

Help will always be available for you in one way or the other if you look for it. It's just the first step that is usually the scariest. Take the step and may the world be with you, guiding you all the way. Life is a learning experience and out of every tragedy in life, we find some valuable lessons. Even when we tell ourselves we cannot handle it, we are often surprised by our own actions in times of need. I had never thought I would be able to handle my mother's loss with grace and in the beginning, I tried desperately to convince myself this wasn't happening. But then I busied myself in making plans and managing everything. I decided to stay in the moment instead of ruining it by worrying about the unforeseeable future. And that is what gave me strength. Her love and affection for me kept me going. And finally, when we had to say goodbye to each other, we were ready. I still miss her every day but there is no regret in my mind as I did for her what I could have. She is gone but I am still following a healthy lifestyle for myself and my kids. Stay healthy, stay safe. I wish you all the strength and good wishes for your journey ahead.

Don't forget, you are commendable. Tell this to yourself every day.

LEAVE A 1-CLICK REVIEW

I would be incredibly thankful if you could take 60 seconds to leave a brief review on Amazon, even if it's just a few sentences. Thank you!

>> Scan the QR below to write a quick review.

A FREE GIFT TO OUR READERS

JUST FOR YOU!

18 ready-to-use templates that you can download, print, and start using right away! Scan the QR code below or visit luna-carter.com

REFERENCES

Abrahms, Sally. (n.d.). *Group Homes Offer Alternative to Assisted Living.* AARP. www.aarp.org/caregiving/basics/info-2020/group-homes.html

Alzheimer's Association. (2019). *Vascular Dementia.* Alzheimer's Disease and Dementia. https://www.alz.org/alzheimers-dementia/what-is-dementia/types-of-dementia/vascular-dementia

Alzheimer's Disease & Dementia Home Page-HelpGuide.org. (n.d.). https://www.helpguide.org/home-pages/alzheimers-disease-dementia.htm

Alzheimer's Society. (2018). *Alzheimer's Society-United Against Dementia | Alzheimer's Society.* Alzheimers.org.uk. https://www.alzheimers.org.uk/

Anderson, Caitlin. (2022 June 28). *June Is Alzheimer's and Brain Awareness Month. Here's How You Can Help.* Long Island Alzheimer's and Dementia Center. www.lidementia.org/june-is-alzheimers-and-brain-awareness-month-heres-how-you-can-help/

Banovic, Silva, et al. (2018). Communication Difficulties as a Result of Dementia. *Materia Socio Medica*, vol. 30, no. 2, p.221, 10.5455/msm.2018.30.221-224.

CAEd, G. W. R. (2020). The Caregiver's Guide to Dementia: Practical Advice for Caring for Yourself and Your Loved One. Rockridge Press. My Book

Caregiver Stress | Office on Women's Health. (n.d.). Www.womenshealth.gov. www.womenshealth.gov/a-z-topics/caregiver-stress#7

Caregiver Tip: Communicating with Doctors—LifeCircles Pace. (n.d.). LifeCircles —A Porter Hills PACE Partnership. https://lifecircles-pace.org/caregiver-tip-communicating-with-doctors/

Choosing a Residential Care Facility. (2022). Alzheimer's Association. https://www.alz.org/media/Documents/alzheimers-dementia-choosing-residential-care-ts.pdf

Cipriani, G., Danti, S., Puchhi, L., Nuti, A., & Florino, M.D. (2020). Daily Functioning and Dementia. *Dementia and Neuropsychologia*, 14(2), 93-102. https://doi.org/10.1590/1980-57642020dn14-020001

Communicating with Someone with Dementia. (2018). Nhs.uk. https://www.nhs.uk/conditions/dementia/communication-and-dementia/#:~:text=Encouraging%20someone%20with%20dementia%20to%20communicate&text=It%20can%20help%20to%3A,to%20speed%20up%20their%20answers

DailyCaring Editorial Team. (2015). 11 Ways to Get Someone with Dementia to Take Medication—DailyCaring. *DailyCaring.* https://dailycaring.com/11-ways-to-get-someone-with-dementia-to-take-medication/

De Georgi, Riccardo, and Hugh Series. (2016). Treatment of Inappropriate Sexual Behavior in Dementia. *Current Treatment Options in Neurology*, vol. 18, no. 41. https://www.ncbi.nlm.nih.gov/pmc/articles/PMC4980403/

Delirium-Symptoms and Causes (n.d.). Mayo Clinic. https://www.mayoclinic.org/diseases-conditions/delirium/symptoms-causes/syc-20371386#:~:text=Delirium%20is%20a%20serious%20disturbance,hours%20or%20a%20few%20days

Dementia Care Practice Recommendations for Professionals Working in a Home Setting Phase 4 Alzheimer's Association Campaign for Quality Care Building consensus on quality care for people living with dementia. (n.d.). Alzheimer's Association, https://www.alz.org/media/documents/pros-working-in-home-setting-4.pdf

Ellison, J.M. (2015, May 25). *Medical Conditions that Can Mimic Dementia.* BrightFocus Foundation. https://www.brightfocus.org/alzheimers/article/medical-conditions-can-mimic-dementia

Fact Sheet: U.S. Dementia Trends. (n.d.). PRB. https://www.prb.org/resources/fact-sheet-u-s-dementia-trends/#:~:text=About%203%25%20of%20adults%20ages,adults%20ages%2090%20and%20older.&text=Women%20are%20slightly%20more%20likely,men%20had%20dementia%20in%202019

Frontotemporal Dementia. (2017, October 20). NHS. https://www.nhs.uk/conditions/alzheimers-disease/symptoms/

Gadgets That Can Help Dementia Caregivers & Ailing Elders-Silver Talkies. (2018). Silvertalkies.com. https://silvertalkies.com/gadgets-that-can-help-dementia-caregivers-ailing-elders/

Genworth. (2018). Cost of Long Term Care by State | 2018 Cost of Care Report | Genworth. Genworth.com. www.genworth.com/aging-and-you/finances/cost-of-care.html

Heerema, E. (2015). *How Dementia Can Make Activities of Daily Living (ADLs) More Difficult.* Verywell Health. https://www.verywellhealth.com/dementia-daily-living-adls-97635

Hoyt, Jeff. (n.d.). Retirement Communities | Senior Retirement Homes & 50 plus Housing. SeniorLiving.org. www.seniorliving.org/retirement/communities/

How to Talk to Someone with Dementia, Alzheimer's, or Memory Loss. (2019). Training.mmlearn.org. https://training.mmlearn.org/blog/how-to-talk-to-someone-with-dementia-alzheimers-or-memory-loss

Huang, H.-L., Chen, M.-C., Huang, C.-C., Kuo, H.-C., Chen, S.-T., Hsu, W.-C., & Shyu, Y.-I. (2015). *Family Caregivers' Role Implementation at Different Stages of Dementia.* Clinical Interventions in Aging. 10, 135-146. https://doi.org/10.2147/cia.s60574

Knowledge and Skills Needed for Dementia Care A Guide for Direct Care Workers. (2006). https://www.interiorhealth.ca/sites/Partners/SeniorsCare/

DementiaPathway/EducationalResources/Documents/ DemCompGuide_181812_7.pdf

Lynch, M. (2022, April 27). *Choosing a Professional/Paid Caregiver*. Americanbar.org. https://www.americanbar.org/groups/senior_lawyers/publications/voice_of_experience/2022/april-2022/choosing-a-professional-paid-caregiver/

Lynn, Alison. (2022). The Criticality of Self-Care by Dementia Caregivers. Americanbar.org. www.americanbar.org/groups/senior_lawyers/publications/voice_of_experience/2022/april-2022/the-criticality-of-self-care-by-dementia-caregivers/

Mayo Clinic. (2018). Mayo Clinic. Mayo Foundation for Medical Education and Research. https://www.mayoclinic.org/

Moreno, Jonathan D., et al. (2010). *Ethical Considerations in the Care of Patients With Neurosurgical Disease*. Edited by James, E. Cottrell and William L. Young. *ScienceDirect*, 5th ed., Philadelphia, Mosby, pp.-425-438. https://www.sciencedirect.com/science/article/pii/B9780323059084100296

Morris, M.C. (2016). Nutrition and Risk of Dementia: Overview and Methodological Issues. *Annals of the New York Academy of Sciences*. 1367(1), 31-37, https://doi.org/10.1111/nyas.13047

National Institute of Aging. (2019) National Institute of Aging. https://www.nia.nih.gov/

Nora, Lois Margaret. (2013). *Law, Ethics, and the Clinical Neurologist*. Edited by James L. Bernat and H. Richard. Beresford. *ScienceDirect*, vol. 118, Elsevier, pp. 63-78, https://www.sciencedirect.com/science/article/abs/pii/B9780444535016000056

Planning for the Future After a Dementia Diagnosis. (n.d.). National Institute on Aging. https://www.alzheimers.gov/life-with-dementia/planning-for-future

Providing a Safe Home Environment for Alzheimer's Patients. (n.d.). Www.agingcare.com. https://www.agingcare.com/articles/how-to-provide-a-safe-home-for-alzheimers-patients-114872.htm

Seladi-Schulman, J. (2021, November 22). *Brain: Function and Anatomy, Conditions, and Health Tips*. Healthline. https://www.healthline.com/human-body-maps/brain#Brain-conditions

Sexual Behavior. (n.d.). Alzheimer Society of Canada. https://alzheimer.ca/en/help-support/im-caring-person-living-dementia/understanding-symptoms/sexual-behaviour.

Social Care Institute for Excellence. (2010). Having a Conversation with Someone with Dementia-SCIE. Scie.org.uk. https://www.scie.org.uk/dementia/after-diagnosis/communication/conversation.asp

Sollitto, M. (n.d.). *Senior Housing Options for Dementia Patients*. Aging Care. https://www.agingcare.com/articles/alzheimers-assisted-living-facility-142284.htm

Symptoms-Alzheimer's Disease. (2022, January 28). NHS. https://www.nhs.uk/conditions/alzheimers-disease/symptoms/

Technology & Devices to Assist Alzheimer's and Dementia Caregiving. (2018). Dementiacarecentral.com. https://www.dementiacarecentral.com/caregiverinfo/technology/

What is Dementia? Symptoms, Types, and Diagnosis. (n.d.). National Institute on Aging. https://www.nia.nih.gov/health/what-is-dementia#:~:text=Brain%20scans.,the%20brain%20and%20other%20organs

Made in the USA
Coppell, TX
31 December 2022